Dare to Believe!

May Rowland

Unity Books
Unity Village, MO 64065

Dare to Believe!
was first published in 1961;
this is the fourteenth printing.

FOREWORD

The articles in this book were written to meet the needs of many people who have written to Silent Unity for prayers. Unity teaches a way of life. It has been my endeavor in this book to give you ideas which will help you to a way of life constructive and uplifting. Your health, your happiness, and your success depend on your thinking, feeling and acting in accord with Truth principles as taught by Jesus Christ.

CONTENTS

Foreword

God Is Your Help in Every Need

M ANY visitors and students who come to Unity Village express themselves in this way: "Being in Unity Village is like being in heaven."

Heaven means something different to each individual, but we think of heaven as a harmonious, uplifted state of mind. You remember Jesus' answer to the Pharisees' question regarding the kingdom of God: "Neither shall they say, Lo, here! or, There! for lo, the kingdom of God is within you."

Visitors enter into a harmonious, uplifted state of mind when they come to Unity Village because it is a place of prayer. Here is the home of Silent Unity. The continuous prayer work going on in Silent Unity releases a feeling of peace and security, a sense of well-being and spiritual uplift, that pervades every part of the Unity work.

As the name *Silent Unity* implies, it

7

identifies a work which is carried on behind the scenes, without outward show, in the deep silence of devout, sincere prayer. The fact that prayer work is going on behind the scenes does not mean that it is a mysterious work. Silent Unity is a ministry of prayer, consecration, and service. It embodies teaching, healing, counseling, and the answering of a volume of correspondence.

With the Silent Unity ministry in mind, Charles Fillmore wrote: "A company of persons gathered in the name of Jesus Christ can build a place in the ether and make it a continuous spiritual battery, from which rays of energy and spiritual substance can be radiated to believing minds anywhere on earth.

"The Christ Mind will take up its abode in such a center of spiritual energy and cooperate with the minds in it in broadcasting health, wealth, and spiritual understanding everywhere."

With the Silent Unity workers in mind, Mr. Fillmore said: "Jesus Christ's men are to be lights that glow and glow with a perpetual current from the omnipresent energy." And this is truly our purpose.

Silent Unity is the great, loving heart of Unity. Its animating spirit is felt throughout the world. Silent Unity's power is from Spirit. It is given divine guidance and direction. Silent Unity has no power except that derived from Spirit. Silent Unity's effectiveness lies in its love for humanity and in its understanding of human nature, as well as in its deep appreciation of the divinity in every man.

Because we do our work with love in our hearts, we are able to get close to the hearts of people. They feel the love in our hearts for them and they reveal their innermost feelings to us. Thus we are able to understand them and help them solve their problems.

This line from the hymn, "Sweet Bells

of Heaven," reveals the close feeling we
have for Jesus Christ:
"I hear the mystic pulses fall
Of One Great Heart that beats for all."

We feel at one with this great heart of
Jesus Christ which beats for all. We feel
at one with the Christ in all humanity.

Because of our long association with
people of every type, we understand their
needs. We know the sorrows, the heart-
aches, the unrest, the disappointments, and
the fears of humanity. We also understand
the aspiration, the heartfelt desires, the innate goodness of mankind. The needs and
the aspirations of humanity are poured out
into this place of prayer every day.

Without intending to, many people reveal their innate goodness to us. They cannot hide their inner feelings and their inner goodness from us because we are interested in their welfare, in their progress,
in their happiness, and in their spiritual development.

When an individual asks the prayers of
Silent Unity, his letters and his telegrams
and his telephone calls are always held as
a secret trust and are kept strictly confi-
dential. Many persons are unable to reveal
their hearts to their families or their
friends, but they feel a need to unburden
themselves. When they are led to come to
Silent Unity for help, they can know that
their thoughts and feelings will be understood, and that we will and do pray with
them without any feeling of curiosity, condemnation, or doubt.

Silent Unity is the loving ministry of
Jesus Christ. Each day we consecrate ourselves to do His will and His work. When
Jesus said: "I go to prepare a place for
you. . . . that where I am, *there* ye may be
also," we believe that He meant a place in
consciousness. We believe that He meant
a place where we are always conscious of
the presence and the power of God working in and through us, a place where we

know God is our help in every need.

Through faithful prayer we have prepared a consciousness of healing, and we recognize Jesus Christ as the head of the Unity work. For many years we have practiced the idea of being lifted to the Jesus Christ consciousness of peace, love, and brotherhood. When we walk hand in hand with Jesus Christ, when we follow His teaching, there is no limit to what we can do in His name.

The people who work in Silent Unity come from every part of the country, from every part of the world. Associated with the Silent Unity work is a training program for student ministers. In this group we have had students from all over the United States, also a German student, several students from Canada and England, three from Japan, one from China, several from Puerto Rico, and a student and teacher from France. These foreign students become a part of the Silent Unity prayer work and they co-operate with us in every way by writing letters in their native language, as well as doing other work in the Silent Unity department.

Those who become associated with this ministry come to us first because of the call of the Spirit; then they are willing to study and work to prepare themselves in the best possible way to do the things that are required of them.

Silent Unity must handle a large volume of correspondence promptly; to do this requires efficiency, as well as a great desire for spiritual development and an understanding of how to serve those who write to us.

I would say the following affirmation is characteristic of the attitude of a good Silent Unity worker:

"I am alive, alert, awake, joyous, and enthusiastic about my work."

Sometimes we have been asked if it is not a little depressing to have the troubles of the world poured out upon us. No, it is not depressing because we know God is a help in every need.

From the early beginnings of the Unity work, the keynote of it has been joy, because Charles and Myrtle Fillmore, who founded this work, thought of prayer as a joyous state of mind. Mr. Fillmore loved to quote this lilting line:

"Let the old world wag as it will,
I will be gay and happy still."

And just as he was a happy man, this is a happy work.

We would be unable to do the work required of us if we merely sympathized with people. We feel deep love and compassion, which are positive attributes of Spirit. We never feel helpless or hopeless, for we remember that "with God all things are possible" and that "the Father abiding in me doeth his works."

We know that the help we give must be known and felt in ourselves. We constantly work in developing ourselves through classes, through prayer, and through discipline in handling our work. Our work is well-organized. At eight o'clock in the morning we meet and read the lesson for that day in *Daily Word*. We then unite in prayer with all persons who are reading the lesson and all who are calling on Silent Unity for prayer help. We also pray at this time for ourselves for wisdom, order, and inspiration in answering our mail.

Prayer has been continuous in the Unity work ever since it was started. Ours is one of the few groups in the world that are organized for continuous prayer. We have regular prayer periods—the *Daily Word* meeting at eight o'clock in the morning, the healing meeting at eleven, a noon prosperity silence, an afternoon meeting of special classes, and another healing meeting at nine in the evening. In addition to these services held each working day, someone is constantly praying in our "room of light," which is known to thousands of people the world over. In this room the light is always shining and someone is always praying. You can turn to the room of light at any time during the night or at any time during the day and receive help in prayer. Hundreds of people tell us that the knowledge of this light in the window, constantly burning, reminds them that someone cares, someone is praying. Wherever they are, they tune in to this continuous prayer and love and feel Silent Unity's blessing.

Though many people do come to Unity Village to study, you need not come to Unity in order to learn to pray with us. We can give you any instruction you may need when you write to us or call us. Co-operation in prayer is essential. God works, not for us, but through us. It is therefore necessary for you to co-operate with us in prayer in order to be benefited. However, when someone is unable to write or call for himself, we gladly pray with him through another individual who is willing to act as a center of faith and make contact with us for prayers.

Many persons go to church on Sunday and feel that they are giving enough time to their spiritual life. But Jesus said: "Give us this day our daily bread," so we appropriate spiritual food every day, through prayer. But our prayer is not always quiet communion with hands folded and eyes closed. We know that "out of the abundance of the heart the mouth speaketh." So we speak words of light, life, peace, and plenty.

We speak these words with power and authority. Even the music of our typewriters is a form of prayer. All day our typewriters are writing out: "God is your light. God is your life. God is your prosperity. God is your happiness. God is your help in every need." Would you not call this an effective form of prayer?

We feel that our prayers are effective because we speak the truth about you. We speak of you as a child of God. We pray that you recognize and accept with faith the goodness of God, which is constantly poured out upon you. We pray that you become aware that the vitalizing, renewing, cleansing life of God in the midst of you is healing you now. We pray that the light of God may shine in and through you to show you what steps you need to take in life. We pray that the justice of God may work in and through your affairs, that you may be prospered abundantly. We pray that you may adjust yourself to meet new situations and conditions easily and harmoniously. Above all, we pray that you may know that God is your help in every need.

We are aware that the Silent Unity ministry is not wholly dependent upon the workers here at Unity Village. Thousands of persons all over the world are an important part of the work. Their prayers are helping us, and our prayers are helping them. Unity people are a great power for good in the world. Ours is a universal work, and all those who pray with us are important in helping the world to gain a more spiritual viewpoint.

Not only can each one of you who reads these words be blessed, illumined, and healed by awakening to the knowledge of the Christ in you, but you can bless and help and heal the multitudes.

We receive thousands of requests for help each week, and also thousands of testimonials of help received. What are the people like who write these requests and these testimonials? They are like you. They are like me. When a worker in Silent Unity has a need for prayer, he sends his name to our prayer room. When I have a need, I send my name to the prayer room, to the "room of light." Every worker has great faith in the spiritual work which is

being done and of which he is a part. If
you were to read the letters on the desks
of the workers at this moment, you might
find: A farmer asking us to pray that his
crops bring a good yield. A little boy asking prayers for his pet that has been lost or
stolen. A mother asking prayers for herself
and her family, that they may have a happy,
harmonious home, a united family. A minister asking our viewpoint about a Bible
passage. A well-known motion-picture ac-
tress asking that she give a good perform-
ance, that she have the strength and en-
durance and health to do a good job. A
government official asking us to pray that
he may use wisdom in fulfilling the duties
of his office. A doctor asking prayers for
his patient.

You may be surprised to learn that the
world is full of praying people. We in
Silent Unity are very happy to be a part of
this great praying group.

The Silent Unity ministry is based on

the charge of Jesus Christ to His disciples:
"As ye go, preach, saying, The kingdom of
heaven is at hand. Heal the sick, raise the
dead, cleanse the lepers, cast out demons:
freely ye received, freely give."

We like to feel that we are helping to
make the teachings of Jesus Christ practical in the lives of all who call upon us.

To follow Jesus Christ is the mission of
Silent Unity, and to do His work as His
disciples is the goal we continually seek to
attain.

[*Dare to Believe!* was written out of the
long experience of May Rowland as the
former director of Silent Unity.]

The Seekers of the Light Are One

HAVE YOU realized that there are people in every nation of the earth who love all humanity, people who are seeking to bring peace, understanding, and brotherhood into the world in which we live? These people are instruments of God wherever they are.

Sometimes as we think of world affairs the outlook seems dark. We see only the working of evil forces and the preparation of instruments of destruction. After all God, who created this world and called it good, is still in charge. Let us align ourselves with this tremendous power of God. Let us co-operate with God in bringing peace, love and understanding into the world in which we live.

It is up to us who live on this planet to learn the first secret of life. We are children of God. And co-operation in expressing Him is essential to our secure, satisfying future on this planet.

One of our loved, familiar hymns is entitled, O Life That Maketh All Things New. It may be in your hymn book. One of the verses and the chorus tell us this:

"From hand to hand the greeting flows;
From eye to eye the signals run;
From heart to heart the bright faith
    glows:
The seekers of the Light are one."

The Chorus:

"United in the Truth we stand,
Proclaiming peace to every land."

In every nation of the earth the seekers of the light are one. It makes no difference what creed or dogma they follow nor what they call their faith. The prayers of all people, seeking the light, unite as a part of the great good of the world.

Sometimes we in Silent Unity are asked to join other peace movements in their activities but we do not feel that this is necessary, because we are all united as seekers of the light. In our unity of purpose we seek ways to bring freedom, justice, and peace into the lives of people the world over.

We, as "seekers of the light," are united in an invisible bond of love for all humanity. We have faith in mankind. We know that good shall be victorious and that nothing can defeat it.

In the beginning God named our world a planet of light. When He said, "Let there be light," there was light. And light is very definitely the keynote of our planet.

Scientists tell us that the energy of this planet is acted upon by light and that any planet, to produce life, must have light. The latent energy in the earth is acted upon by the light of the sun. This produces growth and development in the earth.

The light of the Christ means to man what the light of the sun means to the earth. The seed of man's eternal sonship is within him, and it will grow into a beautiful expression as the light of the Christ nature stirs within him.

The light of man's spiritual nature can turn darkness into light, it can change a barren life into a productive life. Through prayer this change is constantly occurring in the lives of individuals.

We are living on a planet whose nature is light. Light is within us, and all about us. We are truly children of light. Have you ever thought of yourself as a child of light?

You will feel differently about yourself when the light of your spiritual nature sheds its radiance upon every part of your life.

Before the birth of Jesus, the prophet Isaiah said: "The people that walked in darkness have seen a great light . . . and his name shall be called Wonderful, Counsellor, Mighty God, Everlasting Father, Prince of Peace."

Jesus realized that He came into the world as a radiant son of light. You will remember that Jesus constantly identified Himself with light.

"I am the light of the world: he that followeth me shall not walk in the darkness, but shall have the light of life."

And Jesus brought us right into the picture. He did not come to this planet just to show us that He was a light in the darkness, but that the light also is in each one of us.

"Ye are the light of the world. . . . let your light shine before men; that they may see your good works, and glorify your Father who is in heaven."

You can be sure that we are created as children of light, and Jesus came to show us the path of light.

When the light of understanding dawns upon us, it warms us, and love is quickened within us. We commence to respond to the spiritual urge within us to express more and more of the goodness of God.

Just as the light of understanding enabled Jesus to become the prince of peace, so also we can become expressions of love and peace to the whole world.

In the light of understanding there is but one world, one people, all children of God, children of light.

Were we to see the poverty, the frustration, the hardships, and the despair that some of the people of the world suffer, we would want to do all within our power to help them. We do contribute help in a measure, through our government and other organizations. Whatever each of us does to help the peoples of the world, let us do it with warm, loving hearts and sincere prayers so that we may always be fair and understanding of the people in every land.

Benjamin Franklin very beautifully expresses our sentiment about other lands in the following words:

"God grant that not only the love of liberty, but a thorough knowledge of the rights of man may pervade the nations of the earth, so that a philosopher may set foot anywhere and say: 'This is my country.' "

The world can be united through loving, understanding, warm hearts. People at home and abroad respond to love.

Frequently we speak of giving someone our blessing. A blessing is the essence of the highest spiritual realization that we can give to another.

We can give a blessing silently or we can speak it aloud.

In the fall of 1959 I was asked to make some talks to Unity groups in England. They were not large in numbers but they each had great faith in the power of Truth to bless.

I felt I could take a special blessing of love to England, because the day I was to leave by jet plane the *Daily Word* message seemed—as so many of our friends say—just written for this occasion. This was the prayer for the day:

"I love you, I bless you, and I have faith in you."

Silent Unity used this prayer for me. Then we prayed for the people of England. We felt our unity with all our *Daily Word* readers in the various lands throughout the world. We felt that this message of love was encircling the world, and that there was tremendous power in the idea. All *Daily Word* readers were saying to their families, their friends, and to each other: "I love you, I bless you, I have faith in you."

The idea brought out in the lesson was that we do not withhold our love from anyone, we love as God loves.

These ideas prepared the way before us for the work in England.

The response to the idea was warm, loving, and understanding. I felt very close to every person I met in England, not only to Unity friends, but to those whom I met on the streets, waiting for busses, in the hotels and in restaurants. Everyone seemed to be a beloved child of God and acted as though he were.

There was not one discordant note any place on the trip.

"I love you, I bless you, I have faith in you." These are magical words. They will bring you a satisfying, unifying feeling of oneness with all people.

Silent Unity receives letters from people in almost every part of the world. To many people Silent Unity has become a symbol of peace.

One of our dear friends in Greece addressed her envelope to:

" 'Peace on earth, good will toward men.'
Lee's Summit,
U.S.A."

For many years we have printed these words of peace on the back of our envelopes. This friend in Greece was very happy to know that way off in America people were praying for peace for the world.

Silent Unity loves to be thought of as a center of peace. The workers pray daily for world leaders that they may find unity in thought, purpose, and understanding, that they may be inspired to right action for the mutual good of all mankind.

Silent Unity prays daily for the United Nations that they may deal justly and with understanding in relation to all the problems which are presented to them. We bless these leaders and the United Nations every day.

A few years ago a professor of theology came to visit us at Unity Village. He was especially interested in our prayer services in Silent Unity.

He seemed to understand that we would pray for individuals who called upon us for help, but he seemed surprised to learn that an important part of our daily prayer service is to pray for world leaders and for peace and understanding for all nations.

He asked interestedly, "You mean that you keep in touch with things going on in the world and pray for the right outcome in these matters?" Naturally our answer was, "Yes." Daily prayer services for the healing of the nations are one of our great projects.

President Eisenhower said of the United Nations meditation room: "It is the living sign of all people's hope for peace." Mr. Eisenhower was able to extend love, friendship, and good will to the many nations of different faiths because he believes that every man is a child of God.

Let me quote from an interview that Dorothy Thompson had with President Eisenhower in Paris:

"Democracy is indivisible from the idea that man is a child of God, and as such sacred.

"Without this concept that man is a soul and a spiritual being, the idea of human equality would never have come into this world.

"Behind every ideology lies an assumption, an act of faith. That is why there never was and never can be a great and enduring civilization without a basis in religious principles. The most important thing about any man or any society is what it believes in."

In 1955, when I was on a tour of Europe, I was much impressed by an article that was handed to me with my passport. It contained information for bearers of passports, and was entitled "Your Attitude." It read:

"Robert Oppenheimer once said: 'The best way to send knowledge is to wrap it up in a person. Your United States passport gives you the status of goodwill ambassador for our country, and it is primarily through you and other travelers that people in foreign countries know America. Your presence abroad can aid international understanding in helping the United States to be understood.'"

The following part of this article on my passport was taken from a talk by President Eisenhower given in October 1943 in New Orleans:

"Each of us, whether bearing a commission for his government or traveling by himself for pleasure or for business, is a representative of the United States of America, and he must try to portray America as he believes it in his heart to be, a peace loving nation . . . trying to be partners with our friends. And we accept for a friend anyone who genuinely holds out the hand of friendship to us as we do to them."

President Eisenhower often said that we must wipe out prejudice as our contribution toward world peace.

As seekers of the light we all would like to say to people of other nations: "We want peace and friendship, with freedom and justice for all."

The healing of the nations depends upon the healing of the people in the nations and how much they are willing to contribute toward peace.

Each one of us has a special contribution to make toward peace.

During World War II in one of our Silent Unity meetings each one present decided that he would like to make an individual contribution toward peace.

This decision meant that each one of us must cleanse his mind of thoughts of prejudice, intolerance, and all of those attitudes of mind which are a part of the warring consciousness. We knew then, as now, that peace is made up of love and good will, tolerance and understanding.

About this time we commenced using a prayer which in its original form was sent to us by a woman in Australia:

"Almighty Father, let there be peace on earth, and let it begin with me." Silent Unity has changed the last part to read: *"let it begin with love and peace in my*

heart." The next time you feel perplexed about world conditions, use this prayer, and you will find that there is much you can do in your own consciousness.

We all want peace, but usually we want the other fellow to be peaceful first. But all of us are children of God and fully endowed with the ability to live in a friendly, peaceful, harmonious atmosphere of our own making. So we must be willing to contribute our part toward the healing of the nations.

Some people seem to come into the world as harmonizers and peacemakers. They get along with everyone. They hunt for points of agreement with others. When they walk into a room everyone present immediately feels their inner peace, poise, and strength. There are others who have but to walk into a room to agitate most of the persons present.

Every family has its peacemakers and its harmonizers. Likewise, the world has its peacemakers and its harmonizers.

The way to heal the nations is to start in our own consciousness. Let us get in touch with the great spiritual reservoir of love and harmony within us. Then let our harmonious radiance brighten our own homes, let it radiate to our government, and then to the whole world.

Peace begins in the center of our own harmonious consciousness. It starts from the Christ center within us.

Emerson says: "Nothing can bring you peace but yourself. Nothing can bring you peace but the triumph of principles."

No leader, nor group of leaders can thrust peace upon us. It is first an individual matter.

When we get our thinking straightened out, and our hearts filled with love for all humanity, we will be on the way toward establishing the kingdom of God upon the earth.

Emerson further states: "Man is the

word made flesh, born to shed healing to the nations."

Perhaps the reason the nations of the earth have never yet found healing is because the inhabitants have not recognized this great truth, that "man is the word made flesh." When we become more keenly aware of this truth, we will make some tremendous discoveries about ourselves as spiritual beings. We have ignored this gold mine of reality, and now is the time for us to awaken to it.

David Sarnoff, chairman of the board of directors of Radio Corporation of America, and also one of our great inventors, said in an article in Guideposts:

"Material progress is a delusion, unless it is put to the use of eternal spiritual values.

"Every age has its destined duty. Perhaps ours is to develop an awareness of the divine attributes we were given and a sense of responsibility in giving them expression.

Perhaps we are living in a time when a new man is being born, a man of true morality."

He states further:

"We may be a privileged generation who, by taming our fears, our hungers, and our terrible weapons, are asked to pay the price of the transition of the golden age."

Everyone is very important to the bringing in of the golden age.

Jesus Christ is the living symbol of God's good in any form. He took Truth out of the abstract, and made it a way of life. He brought it into the realm of man's experience. Jesus Christ, the Prince of Peace, is the embodiment of all that God is. When we ask in His name we are seeking in the name of the greatest spiritual authority.

We have a great work to do. We believe this planet is under the direction of Jesus Christ, and through the practice of His teachings we can be led into paths of peace, love, understanding, and freedom.

In the nations where Jesus and His mission are not known, understood, and accepted, principles of Truth are revealed to the people by their inspired spiritual leaders. And they are enabled to live by these principles and be led by them into paths of righteousness and peace.

If we are awakened to our importance as children of God, we will do our part in bringing His goodness into the world. We will commence to prove the truth of the scripture:

"He giveth to all life . . . and hath made of one blood all nations of men for to dwell on all the face of the earth."

"And my people shall dwell in a peaceable habitation, and in sure dwellings, and in quiet resting places."

A simple prayer by St. Francis of Assisi, written over seven hundred years ago, puts into words what all "seekers of the light" have in their hearts:

"Lord make me an instrument of Thy
     peace;
Where there is hatred, let me sow love;
Where there is injury, pardon;
Where there is doubt, faith;
Where there is despair, hope;
Where there is darkness, light;
Where there is sadness, joy.
O Divine Master, grant that I may not so
     much seek to be consoled, as to con-
     sole;
To be understood, as to understand;
To be loved, as to love;
For it is in giving that we receive;
It is in pardoning that we are pardoned."

Getting Acquainted with God

"In the life of Omnipresence do I dwell,
'Tis above, around, within me, all is well;
Life divine forever guiding all my ways,
Life divine forever filling all my days."

TRUE PEACE and relaxation come to
him who contemplates the Truth
brought out in this verse. He feels
as though burdens were lifted and all personal care and responsibility have departed
from him.

To think about the nearness of God is
uplifting to our soul and strengthening to
our body. He is around, beneath, within
us as the very essence of our life. Few of
us learn to know Him intimately, for we
spend most of our time thinking about our
temporal needs and seeking to satisfy
them. We busy ourselves with the working
out of all sorts of plans to make our lives
successful and happy. If we could but

turn loose of all that troubles us and trust in the omnipresence of God to fill all our days, we would find the path of unending peace and satisfaction.

If we will be still, cease running here and there, and spend some time in getting acquainted with God as the great Omnipresent One, we will find the source of all that our soul longs for. Through our turning to Him in quietness and in prayer He will reveal Himself to us as omnipresent life, omnipresent love, the omnipresent source of our health, our wisdom, our prosperity, our success.

When we become aware of His omnipresence, the old concept of God as being a man in the heavens, the willful and supreme dictator of our life, just easily and quietly slips away. Our awareness of God as being omnipresent helps us to rest in the peace of His all-infolding presence. We truly realize that "in him we live, and move, and have our being." We cannot

get into any situation where He will not
immediately respond to our call. His promise, given to us through Isaiah, is, "Before
they call, I will answer; and while they
are yet speaking, I will hear." Is He not
very near to us to respond so quickly? With
the mere yearning in our hearts for Him,
He will respond!

A friend who might be ever so near
would not intrude upon our privacy. The
Spirit of God, which is always here, only
awaits our recognition of His presence to
pour out His blessings upon us in overflowing measure.

Man's birthright gives him freedom to
choose whether he will accept or reject so
generous an offer. God is gracious in His
omnipresence; He gives of His life and
substance enough to sustain us until we
learn whence this life and substance come,
and lay hold of them in fuller measure by
giving our attention to their source.

In the peace and tranquillity of your

soul, think about the presence of God. He is never apart from you; just rest in the knowledge that underneath you are the everlasting arms of love bearing you up, protecting and sustaining you, filling your life with joy.

In your heart breathe forth this prayer many times a day:

"In God I live, move, and have my being. He satisfies my longing soul and fills my life with unending joy."

The Answer

IN THE SUMMER of 1950 I traveled through Germany with a group of Americans and witnessed for myself the effect of total war on a nation. To travel through a war-torn country makes one realize that war is never the answer to the problems of the individual or the world.

I had not thought that I would find peace in the midst of a war-shattered country. But in the little town of Oberammergau in Southern Germany there is peace itself, the peace of Jesus Christ. Almost everyone has heard of the Passion play, which is given every ten years to commemorate the sparing of the village from the ravages of plague in 1634. I went to see the play, but I was not prepared for the impact it made on me and on the six thousand other persons who were there from every part of the world.

To be in the village itself is to feel

close to Jesus Christ, for the villagers seem to take on the strength, the goodness, the humility of Jesus. The whole atmosphere is uplifting, peaceful, and comforting. To the people of Oberammergau the Passion play is more than a wonderful spectacle; it is a way of life, for which they are continually preparing themselves. Whoever sees the play feels that the actors live the parts they enact. He feels their strength of character, their depth of feeling for what they are doing, and underneath it all their consecration to an ideal. All through the play he is impressed by the great humility of Jesus, His great understanding, His love for humanity. Whoever sees the play witnesses the positive strength and power there are in humility. He sees the effect of real goodness upon all types of people.

As I sat with the thousands of others from early morning until late at night and watched this moving, wonderful enactment of the life of Jesus, I kept thinking: "This

is more than a historical pageant; this is
the living Truth!"

As I listened to the wonderful words
of Jesus, I remembered a bit of verse that I
learned as a child in Sunday school, one
that has always stayed with me:

"Jesus Christ, make Thyself to me
　　An ever-present reality.
　　More present to faith's vision keen
　　Than even the nearest person seen."

I thought how the Unity interpretation
of Truth has made Jesus Christ an ever-
present reality to me.

I remembered from the teachings of
Charles Fillmore that Jesus Christ made a
rent in the materialistic consciousness and
showed us a way back to God, thus shorten-
ing the evolutionary period of man's development by millions of years.

As the Passion play progressed through
the Crucifixion and the Resurrection, the
thought came to me clearly that Jesus the
man translated His body into pure God-

substance and life. The substance and life of His spiritualized body were changed into mind substance and life, and can be appropriated only through the mind. When I pray and ask in the name of Jesus Christ, the resurrected, eternal Christ, I am appropriating, through the avenue of the mind, that which Jesus Christ is eternally —spiritual life and substance.

Charles Fillmore spoke of this appropriation as a spiritual transfusion. As I sat in the quiet and intent audience, some of them so moved by the spectacle that tears streamed unnoticed down their faces, as I listened to the exalting music, as I felt the spiritual upliftment, I thought, "All of us here are experiencing this mystical transfusion, all of us are appropriating the Christ into ourselves."

In cities close around Oberammergau was the rubble and ruin of war, but there in this little mountain village was the answer to war, and in the hearts of thousands who had traveled here the words of Jesus Christ were being clothed again with power and faith.

The only answer to war is the spiritualization of the minds of men. The answers to the problems that confront us as individuals, and as one world, can only come through an awakening of the spiritual nature of man.

There has always been within man a vague yet persistent feeling that there is something within him which is greater than he expresses. However, he has not given this something freedom to express itself because he is not sure of himself, and because he is bound by the objective world of appearances. Not until the coming of Jesus Christ was the way clearly pointed out that would lead to the discovery of the spiritual nature of the individual. Jesus knew His divinity. Jesus knew that within each man there is the divine spark, the Christ. Jesus' purpose was to reveal this powerful truth to man.

God spoke through the early day prophets and inspired leaders for the purpose of
awakening mankind to that which was
written in each heart. You remember that
Jehovah spoke through Jeremiah, the
prophet, and said: "I will put my law in
their inward parts, and in their heart will I
write it."

Jesus Christ came teaching, "Ye shall
know the truth, and the truth shall make
you free." The truth which Jesus taught
must come alive again in our mind and
heart so that it becomes an active working
power in our daily living.

The answers, which come through seeking Truth in prayer, keep us from deterior-
ation and destruction. These right answers
teach us to build constructive lives and a
harmonious world.

Jesus Christ came to show us a way of
life, and the way that God fulfills Himself
through us. His teachings were meant to

be understood by everyday people like you and me. Perhaps our minds have become confused by the teachers of Christianity who have made our religion so complicated that we do not understand it.

Perhaps we are like the German university student who said of his professor: "My professor is a very learned man, very learned indeed. He is so learned that in ten minutes he can make the simplest subject completely incomprehensible. With him, therefore, the more I learn the less I know."

Emerson beautifully phrased his thought concerning the mission and purpose of Jesus Christ with these words: "Jesus Christ belonged to the true race of prophets. He saw with open eye the mystery of the soul. Drawn by its severe harmony, ravished with its beauty, he lived in it, and had his being there. Alone in all history he estimated the greatness of man. One man was true to what is in you and me. He saw that God incarnates himself in man, and evermore goes forth anew to take possession of his World. He said, in this jubilee of sublime emotion, 'I am divine. Through me, God acts; through me, speaks. Would you see God, see me; or see thee, when thou also thinkest as I now think.' "

The Flame of Faith

ARE YOU acquainted with the power within you that will remake your life?

This power within has been known and used by the sages of every generation. It opens closed doors, it reveals hidden secrets. You are not ruled by a power that is outside you. Your life is ruled and governed by a power that is within you.

You exercise the right to use this power through your faith. Faith is God's gift to man. It has established an eternal bond between you and the power within you, the power that created you.

Are you living your life without being aware of the living bond between you and God? If you are, your faith may be like a dying ember. If you feel that all the good things of life bypass you, if you feel that nothing works out right for you, and if you are discouraged and depressed, these feelings are surely indications that your faith needs to be stirred until it flames and brings you again into the pathway of light.

When you see by the light of faith, you become aware of the tremendous power that you can exercise—power that pours in and through you from your source, God.

Faith aroused glows and flames within you. It releases healing, restorative forces within your body temple. It renews and rebuilds your body and gives you the feeling of youth and vitality. It stirs the energies of your being, and you become enthusiastic about living. Joy enters into your actions, and you are happy and uplifted. You feel unbound and free and you enter upon a path of achievement. Nothing stands in your way; every phase of your life is brightened.

Faith acquaints you with the power that is hidden from the reasoning mind. It reveals itself to you as a feeling of oneness with the eternal good. It gives you the courage to become the all-conquering man. It arouses the spiritual self within you.

When faith becomes a flame in man's mind, he sees by the light of this flame that there are no impossible situations. He knows that there is a way through every difficulty.

Faith is rapidly becoming a tremendous working factor in the minds of our scientists, who are opening great vistas of knowledge and enlarging our horizons. We are becoming acquainted with the heavens. Many people are speculating about the possibility of interplanetary travel. Faith is a pioneer quality of the mind, and it loves to explore the unknown. Faith illumines the way, it dares to go beyond that which it sees.

Every time I take a trip across the country in one of the great planes I think of ingenious man. I bless him for his faith, courage, and accomplishment. Then I remember Peter walking on the water, be-

coming fearful, and being taken into the
boat. Yet walking on water is really no
greater act of faith than flying a plane into
the skies.

Peter's failure to walk on the water and
his turning to Jesus Christ indicate the direction man must take to quicken his faith.
Peter had not as yet awakened to the Christ
within himself. Like Peter we need to learn
of the powers and possibilities that are ours
as sons of God.

It is true that Peter's faith wavered,
but he gained strength through his experience. It was not long until Peter recognized
Jesus as the Christ, Son of the living God.
This ability to discern the Christ developed
even greater faith in Peter.

All of us must act on our faith. If at
first we are not successful, we keep right
on trying. In that moment when we recognize the divinity planted within us we will
know that we are sons of God, sons of the
Most High. We will then understand what

Paul meant when he said, "Christ in you, the hope of glory."

From this high consciousness of our sonship we commence to work in accord with our faith, and no matter how many challenges there are to our faith, nothing shall prevail against it.

Healing is accomplished through this high recognition of man's divinity. When you want to help some individual, do not think of him in his physical weakness, but think of him in his spiritual strength as a son of God.

God created man in His image and likeness. Think of yourself as being God's image and likeness. This may be pioneering to you, but the flame of your faith will reveal the Spirit of God within you. The way to realize your sonship is not to continue in mistakes, but to accept your birthright as God's child and act accordingly.

When we make man the field of our discoveries and turn our talents to developing him instead of turning all of our talents to developing things, we shall live in a more balanced world. We shall learn to live at peace in ourselves. We shall then have the assurance of being able to live at peace in this world and not be destroyed by our own inventions.

This is not a period in the world's experience, nor in our own, when we can bypass our spiritual development and let our faith lie dormant. While we are learning to fly into outer space, we should also be learning to conquer ourselves so that we shall be able to attain great spiritual heights. Then we will enjoy, not destroy, the peace of outer space. Through conquering ourselves we shall learn to live at peace with all nations.

A medical scientist states that man is a self-renewing mechanism. Should we not learn something about this self-renewing mechanism? Should we not put ourselves in tune with the self-renewing power? If

we kindle our faith, we learn that we are
more than a self-renewing mechanism, as
wonderful as this is; we learn that God,
who is in us, keeps the mechanism in oper-
ation.

We are learning how to live longer.
We know about self-renewal. Let us, then,
not allow ourselves to become old and de-
crepit. Self-renewal has been accepted and
known through the ages. But Jesus was the
only individual we have knowledge of who
was so at one with His source that He
could prove self-renewal. He did this in
overcoming death, and He promised that
whatever He did we can do.

Any great work or achievement of ours
is started in the quietness of our own being
when we let the inspiration of the Christ
Spirit within us awaken, arouse, and inspire
us. When a greater faith stirs within us we
shall find ourselves making greater progress on every path of life. A greater faith
depends on a spiritual quickening to put

it into action. Then it takes hold of spiritual ideas and makes them work. With a greater stir of faith we feel a greater urge to develop our God-given powers and to help others develop theirs.

Faith is never passive. "But be ye doers of the word, and not hearers only, deluding your own selves." Do not just listen to me or to anyone else. Get busy; use your ideas. Too many of us excuse ourselves by thinking we do not have enough understanding to apply the ideas we have. Do not delude yourself, get busy.

Sometimes we say, "If I just had enough faith I could be healed," or, "I could get a better position," or, "my life would be happier," or, "my husband would quit drinking," or, "my children would treat me better."

To develop a greater faith let us apply to our own lives what Paul said to the Romans: "So then faith *cometh* by hearing, and hearing by the word of God." Paul does not mean that you should always be listening to what someone else says, someone like your minister or your good friends. He means that you are to use the word of God and to listen to it yourself. He does not mean that you are just to go to church on Sunday and listen to a minister, but he means that you are to let your mind and heart be quickened by the words of God that you yourself speak. You are to use your prayers, and listen to them with an inner, listening ear.

Have you ever listened to your own affirmations or prayers, or do you repetitiously go over your affirmations and prayers without listening to them? Many times it is hard for us to attune ourselves to the prayer affirmations we are making. We read in Romans: "The word is nigh thee, in thy mouth, and in thy heart: that is, the word of faith, which we preach." We do then preach faith.

When we speak words of prayer, they

are supposed to be the truth about us as children of God. For instance, use a simple word of prayer like this: *"I work without weariness, for I love God and serve His highest purpose in my life."*

How many wonderful, faithful souls have said such a prayer time and time again, perhaps in different words, but with a consecrated spirit, and have found that they could do twice as much work as before! This was because their inner listening ear was open and receptive to what they said in their words of prayer.

Back of the increase of faith is practice of the art of prayer every day.

When we try to overcome a condition in our life and seem to make no progress, it is because we have not sufficiently increased our faith through prayer. Remember, faithfulness to prayer must be practiced daily, not just when we have problems to meet. Any artist or musician must learn and continually practice certain tech-

niques in order to be skillful in his pro-
fession. Every human being, to be successful in living his life, must practice the simple art of prayer. "A wise man . . . built
his house upon the rock." This rock is the
rock of faith. On the rock of faith your
life is built.

Every time you pray, every time you
speak a word of prayer, you are building
your life upon the stable foundation of
faith.

Everything in the progress of the race
began with what was at first an infinitely
small amount of faith. You remember that
Jesus did not talk about large amounts of
faith. He spoke of the mustard seed of
faith, and by His illustrations showed what
great power there is in a small amount of
faith.

Read these words of Jesus: "If ye have
faith as a grain of mustard seed, ye shall
say unto this mountain, Remove hence to
yonder place; and it shall remove; and

nothing shall be impossible unto you."

Perhaps you, as I, have read this passage many times and have concentrated on the thought of that tiny grain of mustard seed having the ability to remove mountains. But the important part of that text is the word *say*. We are not just to think, or even just to sit quietly and pray, but we are to speak the word of faith fearlessly as an active, commanding prayer.

One spring there was a tornado in the vicinity of Unity School, and in the vicinity of my home. The radio reported the direction in which it was moving. Those of us at my home were in its direct path, and the tornado was headed our way at a speed of fifty miles an hour. Then the radio and the lights went off. We continued to pray, and also to watch out of the windows of my home. In another few minutes the formidable, black monster with fire seeming to come out of it—because of the glare of the red skies behind it and the flashing of the purple lights from the breaking power lines beneath it—was practically upon us. In the great need and urge of the moment I said to this oncoming monster: "Dissolve in the name of Jesus Christ!"

It was not just I that spoke; it seemed that I was the very mouthpiece of God speaking to this thunderous monster. And, of course, not only was I praying but everyone at Unity School was praying. The result of the experience was that though we could feel the tremendous pull of the whirling wind of the tornado, it turned sharply and took another course. On its way it continued to destroy, but in ten minutes or less when we went outdoors to see what had happened to it, there in the sky it was turned into a thin, white funnel, still holding its shape but with its power gone.

I have witnessed the power of the spoken word of faith through the ministry of Silent Unity. I have witnessed the healing of every type of inharmony of mind, body, and affairs. Why everyone does not receive healing every time he prays, we do not as yet understand. We all would wish we had a great enough faith to save everyone who might be in danger. I am sure that as our faith increases by use we will understand not only how to protect ourselves but how to protect others as well. We are working on building just such a faith.

No matter how big an experience may seem, affirm the Truth in regard to it. Use your faith, no matter how small it may be. Speak your word of prayer with conviction. The prophet Hosea said to the Israelites, "Take with you words, and return unto Jehovah." Speak words that glow with faith and with promise of the good to be accomplished. Use your faith-filled words without fear. Sometimes we fear what others may think about us, or we run away from the problem that should be met.

Jesus' words showed that He was always fearless. When He saw the paralyzed man at the pool, He simply said, "Take up thy bed, and walk." His was not a long, wordy prayer. The flame of faith was back of it, and the man walked. The long prayer may be a part of your meditation. But when there is a call to action, speak your word with power and authority in the name of Jesus Christ.

Why be so meek and mild before the power of God? Remember the words of Jehovah, spoken through Isaiah: "Concerning the work of my hands, command ye me."

When we see that something destructive is happening, it is our God-given right to command the good to come forth. Faith stirs to action our confidence to give the command.

Do you cringe before some so-called incurable disease, or do you have the courage to say, "I will not accept this verdict.

Be thou made whole in the name of Jesus Christ."

Fear keeps us from doing things, and faith helps us to accomplish the so-called impossible. In "Measure for Measure" Shakespeare wrote:
"Our doubts are traitors,
 And make us lose the good we oft might win
 By fearing to attempt."

The world does not need our doubts and fears. It needs our faith. Fear sometimes becomes paramount. Darkness seems to be on the face of the earth, but an active faith in the power of God, the good, blazes a path of light across our horizons. We see things from an enlightened viewpoint. Fear is dissipated. Darkness vanishes from the face of the earth.

Throughout the world persons are rekindling their faith and making it glow. Though the world is now being challenged by appearances of evil conditions, this is not new. Man has always been challenged, but he has been able to meet the challenge through faith. He knows in his heart that everything works together for good, for he is the all-conquering son of God.

We rekindle our faith by daily devotion to the spiritual and uplifting side of life, and to the developing of the divinity in man. Every day we should pray, every day we should use in our individual lives all the faith we have at the moment. Every day our faith increases through the law of use.

Let your heart flame with faith, and others will be warmed in its glow. Enthusiasm for life will be rekindled, and the confidence to command good to come forth will be aroused.

Keeping in Tune

A SPIRIT of harmony pervades the universe. In an address entitled "New Science and New Faith," Donald Hatch Andrews, professor of chemistry at Johns Hopkins University, says, "We are making the startling discovery that, in a word, the basic reality of our universe is not matter but music." He tells us further that if we could attune our ears to listen to what goes on inside the atom we would "become aware of music like great rolling organ music all about us, intermingling melody and harmony. One atom sings and it is answered by music in all the neighboring atoms. It is in this music that we find the real significance of life and the significance of the universe." It is good to think about this vast symphony at the very center of our being. When we quiet our thoughts, our minds, and our bodies, we can feel the spirit of harmony.

This spirit is omnipresent—within, without, and all about us—but we come in touch with it first within our own hearts. To keep in tune with it means not only peace of mind, but it also means perpetual health for the body and joy for the spirit.

To keep himself in tune with the great divine harmony of life is the most important business of man. Above the strife and din of existence, there is always the eternal, heavenly symphony. At any time, under any circumstance, we can feel the peace of its divine melody. It is here just as the air is here. All that is required of us to enter into its sweet harmony is that we open our mind and heart and find the joy and peace that we so much desire.

Pythagoras, the great Greek philosopher, went to Egypt and stayed twenty-one years learning occultism. When he returned to his home, he preached some strange doctrines. Man, he said, and the whole universe were created by God as a musical production. He pointed out that if sand is placed on a plate, and a cord is drawn across the plate, the sand will arrange itself in symmetrical forms. He said that probably the earth took form from the harmonious vibrations of the Word. It may be that God is singing the universe into expression this moment.

Because we are part of this great "musical production," when our sense of harmony is lost we find our body unstrung and we call such conditions sickness or disease; we are momentarily out of tune. Discord in our life and affairs easily passes when we are attuned to the divine.

We do not allow the discord in the lives of others to disturb us and hinder us from seeking to keep our own life in tune. We regulate our life by the perfect standard of harmony. If we listen to the discords that another person is making while getting his life in tune, we can never hope to regulate our own life harmoniously.

Jesus gave the key in these words: "What *is that* to thee? follow thou me." This bidding, "Follow thou me," points the unmistakable way to healing, to abundant life in Christ.

If a person keeps in tune with the good and the true, he will help his neighbor swing into perfect rhythm, and both he and his neighbor will become part of the universal symphony. Health, happiness, and prosperity, indeed all of life's rewards, come to us through our keeping in tune with the infinite harmony of God.

Our keeping in harmony with God makes us perfect instruments for the expression of His mighty word through us. Charles Fillmore says, in speaking of the relation of mind to music: "Who shall tell what man may do when all his forces are brought into play, and he knows how to properly control them. When the faculties are in spiritual harmony, music flows from man as naturally as the brook murmurs in cadence or Niagara roars in organ tones."

All the beauty that we behold and all the melody that we hear come to us because of our attunement with the spirit of harmony. Both beauty of character and loveliness of face emanate from an inner peace that results from attunement with infinite Spirit.

Words like these from Shakespeare help to create the feeling of quietness and to put us in touch with the beauty of life: "How sweet the moonlight sleeps upon this bank!
Here will we sit, and let the sounds of music
Creep in our ears; soft stillness and the night
Become the touches of sweet harmony. . . .
Look, how the floor of heaven
Is thick inlaid with patines of bright gold:
There's not the smallest orb which thou behold'st

But in his motion like an angel sings,
Still quiring to the young-eyed cherubins;
Such harmony is in immortal souls."

Sometimes we feel that we could live more harmoniously, with less confusion and disorder in our lives, if we could change our environment. However, changing one's environment is not the solution to the problem, though it may be a temporary help.

In the study of Truth we recognize that our environment is an outpicturing of our states of mind. Naturally we carry our states of mind with us wherever we go, and in entirely different surroundings we would still have the same type of problem to meet that we have now.

In order to change conditions in our environment we must change our own consciousness. We start to change conditions by overcoming the state of mind that binds or limits us. Then we cultivate the harmony and peace and love we desire.

Paul, in his ministry, refused to be in bondage to trials and tribulations. He took the positive stand: "None of these things move me." This is a good place to begin in freeing ourselves from the states of mind that bind and limit us.

States of mind are not altered by changes in circumstances and surroundings, but circumstances and conditions are altered by changes in our states of mind.

The solution to man's every problem is in man's own consciousness. When we learn to tune in to universal harmony through daily prayer, we find new joy in living. Our body responds with harmony and health, our mind is at peace, and our affairs are in order.

Knowing the importance of keeping our lives in tune, let us be joyous, let us be happy and enthusiastic about the good things in life. Let us put into action the joyous life and energy within us by talking and thinking about the good things. Let us give thanks to God for the blessings that we daily receive. Let us bless with our love and good will the persons with whom we are associated; let us find joy in loving service.

We can live in such harmony with the Infinite that we need not suffer pain, we need not know sickness. Is not this state worth attaining? Let us enter into the joyous, harmonious state of mind that will make us healthy, keep us healthy, and fill our lives with peace and happiness.

Give It the Light Touch

W E ALL know the light touch of a spring breeze, and we enjoy it and are refreshed by it. Many of us also know the cold blast of winter, and we are not fond of its fury.

Sometimes we attack our problems with the fury of a winter storm, but let us remember that it is the light touch of the warm spring breeze that dissipates the snow and breaks up and dissolves the ice.

Friends who are weighed down with problems into which they pour the substance of their time and attention write to Silent Unity. Often, the problems have become so absorbing to the individual that he cannot think or talk of anything else; the disturbing conditions have become almost an obsession.

One of our correspondents discovered that she was doing this. She wrote us: "I thought I could not concentrate, and I found I was concentrating very well—on my problems all day long! Now I can see what you mean when you say concentrate on the peace, harmony, and health you desire."

Many of us do just what this friend did. We concentrate on what we do not want rather than on what we do want. As we concentrate on the good, we are giving that which is not good the light touch. "The light touch" is the touch of light. That is, we let the light of Truth shine into the situation or circumstance to reveal the good and to clarify our thought in relation to it. Prayer enables us to do this.

In practicing the art of prayer we learn to let go the things that bother us. We learn to turn them over to the intelligence of Divine Mind to solve. I mention practicing the art of prayer because it is through continuous practice that this art is perfected. Prayer strengthens us so that we can let go a perplexing situation. This is another way to meet a challenge with the light touch. After all, our success lies not so much in how we handle the situation, but in how we handle ourselves.

We are able to handle each situation that arises easily, smoothly, and harmoniously—with the light touch—when we learn to control and direct our thinking about each situation. Our strength emerges from our way of thought.

Instead of allowing our thoughts to dwell heavily on troubles, cares, and difficulties, let us change the course of our thinking. Let us give these things the light touch. Let us make our thinking positive, and cultivate the habit of putting our full attention on the good. Let us remember what Paul said: "Whatsoever things are true, whatsoever things are honorable, whatsoever things are just, whatsoever things are pure, whatsoever things are lovely, whatsoever things are of good report . . . think on these things."

Thinking on "these things" will allow us little time to think on the things that are not true.

We can learn to change our thinking as easily as we change our clothes. We can turn from a negative thought to a positive thought as easily as we go from one room to another. We can deny the negative appearance and affirm the Truth.

Start by giving any situation that concerns you the light touch. Do not bear down on it like the winter winds. As you give it the light touch in your thought and in your feeling, you will be enabled to give the fullness of your thought and feeling to the healing of the situation.

If you are undergoing a hard experience and things seem to press in on you and you do not know which way to turn, use this prayer: *"The clear, unclouded Mind of Jesus Christ dominates my thinking, my feeling, and my acting."* Concentrate on this truth instead of concentrating on the negation. Work with yourself instead of with the negative experience. Start looking at everything that concerns you in the light of the Christ.

A man wrote to Silent Unity for prayers to help him untangle his affairs. He was a very, very busy man. Everything in his life seemed to be piling up. He could see no way to turn to free himself from the limiting, binding, tense situation that oppressed him. He felt as though he were closed in by a wall.

As Silent Unity prayed with him, he discovered that he had been giving his full attention to the adverse conditions and had been giving no thought to the Power that would bring him release. His freedom came when he turned his attention to the thought: *"I am one with Almightiness. My environment is God. Order and well-being reign in my life and in my world."* With this in mind he was able to relax, to think clearly, and to handle all his affairs with a light touch. The turmoil and the frustration were gone.

Even as we learn to give the light touch to the things that concern us, we can also learn to give them the touch of light. We do this by thinking of the light of Christ as shining into every dark corner of our thinking. We do this by letting the light of Christ reveal the solution to problems, the answers to questions, the fulfillment of our every need.

I Am Part of All That Is Good!

In moments rare there comes to me
  A vision unexpected;
I clearly see within my soul
  The universe reflected.
I am a part of all that's good,
  I feel, I know no limit;
The God in all stands forth so clear,
  No fancied ills can dim it.

No matter what life's future hours
  May hold of earthborn sadness,
I know there comes to me in Truth
  A heritage of gladness
That far transcends all grosser things—
  I've caught the vision glorious:
We are a part of all that's good,
  And good shall be victorious.

                    —*Anna L. Derschell.*

I LOVE LITTLE verses that convey great ideas. Many times when I have had something rather difficult to meet and my mind has seemed almost wholly absorbed in meeting the situation, some beautiful line from a song has come to the rescue, and through it the idea for handling the condition has revealed itself.

The verses used at the beginning of this chapter illustrate what I mean:

"We are a part of all that's good,
And good shall be victorious."

If you will let this idea become a part of your consciousness, it will repay you a thousandfold in peace of mind, in greater faith in the victory of good in every situation.

Words like these—words that have special meaning, words that are familiar— are what we hold to when we are "going around a corner" and when we are moving too fast to stop and think out some new form of words or prayer to express the idea we need at that particular moment.

In the stillness of your own room, take one or two lines from these verses into your thought and into your heart. Teach yourself to feel the truth of the idea:

"I am a part of all that's good,
I feel, I know no limit;
The God in all stands forth so clear,
No fancied ills can dim it."

Then when you confront a crisis in your experience, you will not feel that you are alone; you will find that you continue to be a part of all that's good, and your consciousness of good will be so sure and so strong that you will come through your Gethsemane or your dark hour triumphantly. The good to which you have declared your allegiance will see you through.

You who pray with us in Silent Unity are daily training your minds along positive lines. You implant strong, courageous words in your minds and hearts.

More than once, I am sure, you have

caught "the vision glorious" that you are a part of a tremendous power of good. You and we of Unity are a part of the good that is to be victorious in the world. So are all the thousands of persons everywhere who are praying unselfishly for good for all persons. We have all caught the vision and are trying to live by it.

In an apartment where I once lived there was a very pleasant maid who told me she had learned little verses that were helpful to her, and that as she worked she sang them into every corner of the room. No wonder I sensed such a blessing from my little apartment as I entered it! She told me of the verses she used; they are all constructive, joyous and uplifting. We can sing of our good and sing it into every little corner of our life, if we will to do so.

If in this hour you do not feel that your life is in harmony, if you feel low and depressed, if things seem to go wrong for you, let some little memory verse tune you in to the great universal power of good, let it sweep you into its current until you feel and know that you are a part of all that is good, and good shall be victorious!

Spirit Has a Plan

I HAVE talked with hundreds of persons who needed only the assurance that Spirit has a plan for their lives to give them an entirely different attitude toward life.

It is such a simple idea, yet so comforting and easy to follow once you begin to think about it and accept it.

"Spirit has a plan for my life," which is perfection of mind, body, and affairs.

There is a time for silence and a time for activity. We do not always find ourselves apart from the world; we are not always in the silence of prayer. But many prayer ideas on which we meditate can be carried right along into our active lives. *"Spirit has a plan"* is such an idea.

It is an idea that will come to you again and again as you go about your day's work. You may find yourself humming these words to a little tune. *"Spirit has a*

90

plan, Spirit has a plan, the Spirit has a perfect plan, Spirit has a plan."

In Silent Unity we are asked again and again: "What shall I do? I have to make a decision, and I do not know what to do. Tell me what to do." We always tell the ones who ask this that no other person can solve their problems for them or tell them exactly what to do. If we were to try to tell those who turn to us in Silent Unity for help in prayer exactly what to do in their lives, we should not be giving the highest help possible. We always direct these persons to turn to the Spirit of God within them; we tell them that God has a good and perfect plan for their lives, and He will reveal it to them as they pray for guidance, as they open their minds and hearts to Him.

When God breathed into man the breath of life He put within man the source of wisdom that he can always turn to for right answers. When one eagerly seeks the

advice of others he overlooks the fact that
the wisdom of the ages is in him, and that
Spirit in him has the right answers for him.
The Spirit in each of us has only one project, and that is to develop our spiritual nature, to perfect us in mind, body, and affairs.

Since man is God's greatest project and
His Spirit is within man, this Spirit is what
all of us should turn to in seeking an answer
to the question, "What shall I do?"

Someone has said, "Go first to God,
then to man as God directs." So before
asking your friends, "What shall I do?"
turn first to Spirit within you for the right
direction. You will receive answers that
will surprise you.

After spending wearisome nights and
days planning and figuring and working on
the affairs before you, when you give up
and relax and let go, the right solution to
the question suddenly is at hand.

Learn to turn first to Spirit within you,

then the intellect or the reasoning mind will be quickened. The all-knowing Mind of Christ, which has been within you from the beginning, knows the right answer for you according to your development and experience.

God created us to express His love, His wisdom, and His intelligence. How can we do this unless we turn to Him as the source of love, wisdom, and intelligence? Jesus said, "The kingdom of God is within you." Then we must also come to the conclusion that God is in His kingdom within us.

There is a divine plan for us that far transcends our remotest ideas, and we can, day by day, follow this plan by arousing our spiritual nature. To grow spiritually, to grow happily in meeting life's experiences, we need to seek daily this divine plan. It is not an arbitrary plan, but when we are awakened spiritually we refer everything to it. When we co-operate with the divine plan we discover a way of thinking and acting that is superior to the trial-and-error method. Jesus always recognized the plan or the will of the Father. He said, "Not my will, but thine, be done." Even on the Cross He knew that the divine plan for His life would have to be fulfilled.

But the plan did not end on the Cross; it came to a new beginning through the transcendent Spirit within Him. So daily we pray; we ask that we may understand and be directed by the Spirit of wisdom and illumination, which responds to our seeking and fills us with great inspiration for daily living.

We begin to feel the glory of the kingdom within, and it expands to fill our whole nature with its beauty. We feel that all is right with our world. We follow the divine plan, and our lives flow in accord with it.

It is easy to have a high-powered religion for Sundays and special occasions, but it is our daily living that really counts. Every day we need to remind ourselves that Spirit has a plan for us, a perfect plan. And we need to be willing to work with the plan, to put it into action in our lives.

It helps to take the idea that Spirit has a plan and then to add to it the ideas that come to us as we think about it and follow through on the idea. Our thought about it may go something like this: "Spirit has a plan, a perfect plan. Spirit reveals the perfect plan. I understand the perfect plan. I now accept the perfect plan. I am working with the perfect plan. I now enjoy the perfect plan."

You may need merely to say to yourself, "Spirit has a plan." Or you may need to follow through on the idea, to affirm your willingness to work with the perfect plan, to affirm your ability to understand the perfect plan, to affirm your enjoyment of the perfect plan. You know what you need to let go of in your consciousness; you know what you need to build into your consciousness.

When we accept the idea that there is a plan larger than our own ideas we feel a great release from useless struggle. We awaken to the realization that the very Lord of our being, the Christ Spirit, has a perfect plan for us every step of our way; and if we consecrate ourselves to the fulfilling of this plan, we shall rise above trials and tribulations and commence to enjoy richer and fuller lives.

Love the Conqueror

"BUT FROM thence ye shall seek Jehovah thy God, and thou shalt find him, when thou searchest after him with all thy heart and with all thy soul." Thus spoke Moses to the Children of Israel. Later Jesus Christ put the same thought into these words: "Ask, and it shall be given you; seek, and ye shall find; knock, and it shall be opened unto you: for every one that asketh receiveth; and he that seeketh findeth; and to him that knocketh it shall be opened."

We have been seeking God through the ages in ways innumerable. We have sought Him through this teacher and that teacher and in books and records of all kinds. We have sought Him in this church and that church, expecting Him to be revealed in some mysterious way by the minister. But again Jesus Christ said to us, "Neither shall they say, Lo, here! or, There! for lo, the kingdom of God is within you"; and that is where we must seek Him. Let us seek Him now as love, which will prove itself to us in His inner kingdom.

God so loved the world that He gave us Jesus Christ to reveal to us the Christ Spirit that dwells within us and to awaken us to the magnitude of His love. Jesus Christ knew the love of God so fully that He said to us: "If ye abide in me, and my words abide in you, ask whatsoever ye will, and it shall be done unto you." He was so filled with the love of God that He could say to the man who had been crippled for thirty-eight years, "Arise, take up thy bed, and walk"; and the cripple took up his bed and walked. We are so sentimental in our love that if a command like that were given in our presence we might think it a very unloving thing to say.

But the love that was expressed through Jesus Christ was a very active love, and it did mighty works. It was not sentimental:

it wasted no false sympathy on negative conditions. His love commanded and was obeyed. He did not need to say in words, "I love you, therefore I want to help you." All the love of God in Him was expressed through His words, "Arise, take up thy bed, and walk."

We can seek for God as wisdom, God as supreme power, as undeviating law, as never-failing principle, but first let Him become to us the God of love enthroned in our own heart. We shall then know that there is nothing to fear in His law, for His love is just and forgiving. There is nothing to fear in His absolute power, for He is also absolute love. He is the changeless principle of love that is always good. He is not a God of impulses who sometimes wills good and sometimes evil for His children. Can you conceive of a God of love willing sickness, poverty, and even death for His children in the face of this teaching: "For God sent not the Son into the world to judge the world; but that the world should be saved through him"?

Let us not abide in inharmonious self-made conditions, imagining that God so wills. Let us rise up out of this error belief, my friends. Never does the God of love that we know at Unity will for you anything but what He is Himself, absolute perfection. He wills not only that we may be perfect in our spiritual nature but that His perfection may become expressed in our body and in our affairs.

Let us frequently quiet our outer thoughts and activities and really seek Him in the stillness within our own heart.

When you touch the love of God in your heart you find yourself wanting to do something to bless and help others, even as Jesus Christ did. The more you give out of this wonderful gift that is yours the more of heavenly blessings will come back to you.

The Irresistible Power of Divine Love

WHEN YOUR heart is filled with love you will not be critical or irritable, but you will be divinely irresistible.

This is the thought conveyed by a Truth lecturer whom I heard a number of years ago. The speaker was very dynamic, and thoroughly impressed his message upon the minds of his audience. The lecture made such an impression upon me (though I was only a child) that the theme has repeated itself many, many times in my mind and has kept me from being critical and unhappy about inharmonious conditions.

At first the idea of being divinely irresistible sounds rather sentimental and one feels hesitancy about claiming to be divinely irresistible. We associate the idea with the thought of personal attractiveness but, after all, true personal attractiveness is dependent upon something deeper than

101

mere externalities. Unless there is depth of
character and spirituality there is no
strength or drawing power in mere personal attractiveness. But when love fills the
heart it reflects not only in the face, but
also in the very life of the individual; the
beautiful one becomes more beautiful and
the one who lacks beauty and regularity
of features is so lighted up by the radiance
of the inner glow of love that he too becomes divinely irresistible.

To what do we wish to become irresistible? To the real, the true, the good things
of life, do we not? By our ugly, cross,
irritable, impatient thoughts we build up
a wall of resistance to the good that we so
much desire, and then we wonder why we
are not happy, why we are not prosperous,
why we are not making good in our posi-
tions. When we are in a state of irrita-
bility, good cannot possibly be expressed
in our lives. We have failed to let love express itself, and without love there can be

no real happiness, no real success.

There is the individual who thinks that the world has treated him very badly, that no one understands him, that no one likes him, and that everyone is against him. You have heard persons say that. You have heard someone say that a particular person was trying to keep his good from him. How absurd is such a notion! Only a person's lack of insight, his lack of love and understanding, can make him think that even a moment. The only thing that works against anyone is his failure to express the love of God. When a person cultivates the love of God and is willing to let it express itself through him, he finds his life easily and quickly freed from the confusion caused by the belief that someone else wishes to harm him, to keep his good from him.

Love is an inherent power that if allowed to be expressed in one's life, will transform every inharmony, will transmute every negative condition into part of the harmonious whole. The results of love are always good. Do not confuse sentiment, sympathy, and lust with love. I am speaking of the purified, transcendent power of divine love that expresses itself through you and me when we open our hearts and minds to it, when we recognize and encourage it.

If you feel a lack of satisfaction and harmony in your life, if your life seems hard and the way seems dark, it is likely that you are inhibiting love. The first step in remedying such conditions is to forget about your personal self and to cultivate the irresistible power of love in your life by giving something of yourself in a helpful way to someone else. In other words, cultivate the feeling of love and be in expression that which you would bring into your life.

More often than we realize, the lack of love in our lives is simply the lack of expressed love. A person may feel ever so

kindly toward people, but close himself
in by not venturing to express any of his
good feeling. The desire for love is frequently the need to express love toward
others.

Let love express itself through you toward others by silently blessing them, by
quietly praying that the peace and goodness
of God be poured out upon them.

If one wishes to clear up a misunderstanding, it is not especially necessary, unless one is led to do so, to speak openly.
Silently blessing an individual, knowing
that the love of God is revealing all things
in their true state, and that harmony and
perfect peace are established will clear up
a misunderstanding.

The love of God can do wonderful
things for us; it will imbue our lives if
we permit it to do so. It makes beautiful
and smooth the path that was thorny and
hard. It changes our discontent into harmony and happiness. It satisfies our needs,

and is the irresistible magnet that brings the substance of God into manifestation as our visible daily supply.

Let us change the wording of the first statement in this article and make it a more positive help in our lives. Let us say: *"My heart is filled with love, and I am not critical, irritable, or impatient. I am divinely irresistible."* When you say, "I am divinely irresistible," you are speaking of that in you which is and always will be the most powerful force in the world. Jesus said, "Before Abraham was born, I am." I AM is the name through which Jesus Christ knew Himself to be one with the Father. Through this name we can free our lives from disturbances, from darkness no matter how deep it may seem.

Now let us affirm, *"I am the love of God in expression,"* and thus begin gradually and easily to transcend our human limitations. If you will try this practice for even a short period, you will be surprised to find how easy it is to get the feeling of love. Love is an innate quality in man, and it needs only to be called forth to express all its radiance.

As children of God we must be expressers of His love. If you are not attracting the good that you desire in your life, learn to express love; become a radiating center of love; and you will find that love, the divine magnet within you, will change your whole world.

Think of the forgiving power of love as expressed through Jesus Christ. He was not critical of the woman taken in adultery. He did not condemn her. By the power of God's love in expression through Him He gave her the assurance, "Neither do I condemn thee," and then commanded, "Go . . . sin no more." His forgiving love cleansed her life and set her free. Cannot we be expressers of God's love to the extent that we shall feel no condemnation for those who seem to have fallen short of divine perfection? Can we not by the love of God raise them up and bless them, giving them the courage and strength to strive for something better?

Cannot we be so filled with the love of wholeness and perfection that we can with assurance say to the crippled one, "Take up thy bed, and walk"? Never waste sympathy on sickness or on any other negative condition. Jesus did not. He was a lover of perfection and He kept His vision fixed on it. Negation will cry out for sympathetic attention, but remember that negation is not a part of the one whom you would help. Center your attention on perfection and call perfection forth through the love of God in you.

The love of God does not compromise with weakness. It is strong and courageous; it does not make the way easy for man to stay in a state of negation; it sees and calls into expression the perfection of God.

One who does not sympathize with sickness and condone it is often thought to lack love, but do not be misled—his love is fixed upon the perfection that he wishes to see manifest, and to that vision of perfection he must give all his attention.

True healing is based upon the love of perfection. If you would help another your desire for wholeness must not be compromised by any sympathizing, condescending thought about his suffering. Perfection, wholeness, is made manifest through your giving your undivided attention and love to it.

Love of God and love of the good in His fellow man enabled Jesus to say while on the cross, "Father, forgive them; for they know not what they do."

Love was the all-encompassing idea, the powerful force that helped Him to transcend bodily limitations and bring Himself a threefold being into everlasting perfection. Love was the all-conquering Master within Him that allowed Him to proclaim,

"All authority hath been given unto me in heaven and on earth." Love of perfection made possible His resurrection from the tomb.

This desire to see perfection and wholeness manifest enables Silent Unity to be a channel through which the love of God expresses itself to heal you who ask for help.

We do not see your weaknesses, your failures. We behold your perfection, and in the name of the irresistible love of the Christ we call it forth.

Where Is Holy Ground?

WHERE IS holy ground? "The place whereon thou standest is holy ground." You stand on holy ground, because you are holy.

Most of us shy away from the thought that we are holy. When Jesus said to the Jews, "I and the Father are one," they wanted to stone Him. Even when He said, "Is it not written in your law, I said, Ye are gods?" they could not accept it.

We give much attention to the intellectual man and to the physical man, but we are reluctant to think about or talk about the spiritual man, the God-self of us.

"Neither shall they say Lo, here! or, There! for lo, the kingdom of God is within you." "Know ye not that ye are a temple of God, and *that* the Spirit of God dwelleth in you?" Surely if these things are true, if the kingdom of God is within us, surely if our bodies are temples of the living God, we must be holy in God's sight.

In his book *Talks on Truth,* Charles Fillmore says, "Many have caught sight of the fact that the true church of Christ is a state of consciousness in man, but few have gone so far in the realization as to know that in the very body of each man and woman is a temple in which the Christ holds religious services at all times."

Whether we realize it or not, we stand on holy ground, for the church of Christ is in our midst.

I thought much about these ideas when I had the opportunity of visiting the Holy Land. There are many places in the world that are considered holy, but none of them compares with the Holy Land, because this is where Jesus walked and talked and taught and performed His miracles. In the Holy Land one remembers not only Jesus but all the other great Biblical figures who walked with God, who knew Him as a living and real presence.

Every year thousands of persons from all over the world visit the Holy Land and worship there. And as they worship there they bring to the relics of the past something of their faith in the living Christ.

I am convinced that there is a tremendous potential spiritual power in the Holy Land because of all the faith that has been built into it through the words and teachings of Jesus, through His disciples and followers, through the faith of the wonderful prophets of old, and through the faith of the pilgrims who make their way to its shrines year after year.

All of the Holy Land holds a sort of mystical beauty. When I visited there I felt as though I were getting back home. It seemed natural to stand beside the Sea of Galilee, to walk in the garden of Gethsemane, to see firsthand the places that I had read about and known about all my life.

Two thousand years ago the shore of

the Sea of Galilee was a busy thoroughfare; caravans were constantly going through the Holy Land on their way to Damascus, to Egypt, and to other places in the world. For hundreds of years the Sea of Galilee— which is a lake about fourteen miles long and seven miles wide—was a quiet place. There were no towns of any size or importance around its shores. The hillsides were barren. I like to think of the Galilee of Jesus' day. I like to think of Him as a part of a busy, active world, as indeed He was.

This area which has for so many ages been dormant is now being stirred into new life. Industries and housing units are springing up. The town of Tiberias near by is a resort that is being widely publicized.

Other places in the Holy Land have not changed much in two thousand years. When we think of our own country, we realize that in the passing of twenty-five years, a place can have changed so much that were we to go back we would scarcely recognize it.

The remnants of the olive trees that were there in Jesus' time stand in the garden of Gethsemane. Even the costume of the people has in many instances remained unchanged through the centuries. Along the hillsides in Syria and the Jordan you find the robed shepherds of Biblical times. And the women in their flowing dresses still carry water bottles on their heads, filled from the same wells that we read about in the Bible.

The thought of Jesus as the Good Shepherd has always had deep meaning for me, so I felt particularly drawn to the shepherds on the hillsides of the Holy Land today.

It was natural for Jesus, speaking to the people, to use the shepherd as an illustration: "I am the good shepherd; and I know mine own, and mine own know me

. . . and I lay down my life for the sheep."

In the Holy Land one remembers the wonderful work and teachings of Jesus, and one cannot help but wonder what happened to the living Truth that Jesus gave forth there, what happened to the healing power that found expression through Jesus and His apostles and followers. Why did it seem to die out? How did Christianity get bogged down in narrow religious beliefs? Where did we lose the spirit of Jesus and commence to worship Him as a personality? Where along the way did we lose sight of the truth that we are to follow the Holy Spirit that was to come in the name of Jesus Christ, the Holy Spirit He told us about when He said, "I go unto the Father . . . And I will pray the Father, and he shall give you another Comforter, that he may be with you for ever, *even* the Spirit of truth . . . the Comforter *even* the Holy Spirit, whom the Father will send in my name, he shall teach you all things, and bring to your remembrance all that I said unto you"?

The Truth is still the same living Truth that Jesus gave to us, but it became bound in ceremony, form, and tradition. The Truth of Jesus Christ never died out. It has always been alive and vital. It was only through our lack of understanding that our religious beliefs became narrowed down, leaving out the vital Christ teaching. We lost sight of the real meaning of Jesus' teaching when we commenced to worship the man instead of following the great teaching He was giving us. We feel that the man Jesus was saving us without our needing to do anything ourselves. We must learn to worship in spirit and in truth.

Although in the Holy Land we are carried back to the days of long ago as we visit the old shrines and historical spots, it is really the living Christ Spirit that matters. And it seems to me that all over the world the teachings of Jesus are com-

mencing to come into their own in a much
more practical and logical way. People are
commencing to find that the principles that
Jesus taught are sound and living principles, that to follow these principles is the
only way to peace and life.

We do not have to go to the Holy
Land to find the living Christ Spirit for
it is here, everywhere, ever within us. We
only have to go to the Lord of our being
in silence and in prayer.

"Hold, there! Where runnest thou? Know,
        heaven is in thee.
Seekest thou for God elsewhere, His face
        thou'lt never see.
In all eternity, no tone can be so sweet,
As where man's heart with God in unison
        doth beat."

Where is holy ground? "The place
whereon thou standest is holy ground," for
you are holy. Holy ground is truly wherever the Spirit of God is, and He has made
your heart His dwelling place.

Resurrecting Our Ideals

D EAR FRIEND, how long has it been since you thought of yourself as glorious? As splendid? As beloved? As strong and well and capable?

How long has it been since you thought of the world as a beautiful place in which to grow and to work and to play?

How long has it been since you affirmed with joy and faith, "Through the power of Christ within me I can be as wonderful as I want to be"?

How long has it been since you beheld yourself and your associates as freed from limitations, capable of greater growth and of bigger achievement?

It should not have been long since we thus renewed ourselves, but if it has been, now is the perfect time for us to make a fresh beginning.

Our remembrance of our brotherhood with Jesus Christ stirs in us a deep con-

fidence in the divinity of man and his
ability to be glorious, splendid, free. Our
remembrance of Jesus' great courage and
faith awakens in us a determination to revive all the high ideals that we have ever
cherished in our heart.

No matter how discouraged we may
have become, we must never give up our
ideals. We know that we should not. The
Christ in us continuously prompts us to
keep the high vision, and to keep it regardless of appearances, of circumstances.

If our ideal is perfect health and we are
not showing forth health in our bodies, let
us revive our ideal now. Let us take new
hope. Let us not weaken ourselves by
doubting. Instead, let us gain strength by
believing in what we want, by believing
in perfect health. "God saw everything that
he had made, and, behold, it was very
good." The wholeness in which we were
created is still the true nature of our being. Let us revive it and henceforth see our-

selves only as God sees us, saying often:

"I see myself as God sees me, glorious, splendid, beloved, strong and well and capable."

If our ideal is efficiency and we are clumsy at our work, let us believe that we can become efficient. If our ideal is heroism and we have acted the coward, now is the time for us to renew our efforts to overcome fear. Whenever we are tempted to belittle ourselves in any way, let us say:

"Through the power of Christ within me I can be as wonderful as I want to be."

If our ideal is an improved standard of living and we are not receiving enough income to meet our needs, let us not despair. Let us not grow bitter or sink down in a morass of self-pity or say that the world is against us.

Let us instead revive our ability to serve, to forgive, to laugh, to get along with people. Let us revive everything in ourselves that makes us productive and of value to the world, saying often:

"I see the world as a beautiful place in which to grow and work and play. Through the power of Christ within me I revive my ability to live happily, to give good service generously, and to inspire those who, with me, are growing and working and playing."

We realize that we become more and more helpful to our associates as we succeed in resurrecting our own ideals. We recognize that our first work is with our own self and not with the other fellow. We know from experience that we do not help another by insisting that he conform to a set of ideals that we love but that he may not care about. We see that God is working through each person, inspiring him to resurrect his own ideals.

We rejoice in the truth that as we resurrect and follow our own highest aspirations we automatically become an inspiration to others. We are free from the thought that others must follow exactly our own spiritual program. We perceive that standards and ideals vary with individuals. We know that we can do much more toward the uplifting of our associates by making our daily life an inspiration than we can by being a preacher of ideals.

We remember that even Jesus, whose mission was to lead men in the way of overcoming, did not set up Himself or any individual as an example for all to follow but clearly directed: "One is your master, *even* the Christ." Jesus lived as He was directed by the Spirit of God within Him, by the Christ.

Let us listen often to the promptings of the Christ, the Spirit of God within us. Let us revive our faith in the divinity of people and see them freed from all limitations, capable of growth and of greater achievement. Let us gain a deeper respect for each individual's right to freedom of thought and action, freedom to work out his life's purpose according to his own inner light.

Many times we have heard people say: "I have tried so hard to help my husband," or "I have tried so hard to change some of my wife's ideas," or "I have talked and talked to my family, and yet not one of them seems to want to improve." We shall do well to discard the feeling that it is our responsibility to exercise absolute power over our friends or our family. Let us know the truth that the only individual in the world we have the right to work with is ourself. If we keep our own spiritual ideals alive and aglow, then and then only are we a great power in the world for helping others. Even our children respond to our guidance more readily when they see that we are very much the way we talk.

We know that the beliefs easiest to pass on to others are those which are already making us a little more agreeable to live with, a little more fair in our dealings, a little more honest and just in all the relationships in our life. Let us therefore not be more eager to share a belief than we are to live up to it. For instance, if we want to voice strong convictions about peace, let us now revive the ideal of peace that is implanted in our heart. Let us resurrect in our own individual consciousness the emotions of love, tolerance, patience, and harmony.

We can contribute to the peace of the world by keeping our mind stayed on peace, by being peaceful, by controlling our disposition. Instead of condemning others for not giving us peace, let us heed the urge from within us to resurrect all the harmonious qualities of our mind and heart by becoming a creator of peace. Let us say often:

"I accept peace from within myself, from God. I open the way for greater peace by letting go of all tendencies to hate, to condemn, to find fault, to become disturbed and use unkind, bitter words. I remember

the Christ and the Christ way, forgetting all else."

In the name of the Christ, let us rededicate ourselves to our ideals. Let us dismiss the thought that we have in any way impaired our opportunity to be as wonderful as we want to be. The Christ Spirit in us is unchanging—strong, mighty, clean, and pure. We can identify ourselves with it rather than with any shortcoming or unpleasant experience of the past. We can accept now the good role of peacemaker by letting love rule our spirit and our relations with our family, with our friends, with everyone.

Now is the perfect time to revive our ideals, to lift up our vision, to acknowledge our own at-one-ment with God, All-Good.

Make Joy a Habit

EVERYONE wants to be happy. We know that the majority of people are eager to find happier ways of life.

Many persons are unhappy because they have not yet learned the art of living happily and joyously in spite of conditions and circumstances in their lives. But true happiness can be attained by anyone. Every one of us can learn to make joy a habit.

I like this text from James: "Count it all joy, my brethren, when ye fall into manifold temptations." Most of us count the trials instead of the joys of living. It is possible for us to count just the joys of living and forget, or at least minimize, the trials so that we can break our bondage to them.

Jesus said, "These things have I spoken unto you, that my joy may be in you, and *that* your joy may be made full." Joy is inherent in our soul but we must develop it. All of us relate joy to the things that happen in our lives rather than trying to find the source of joy within us. The joy of the Lord is a wellspring within that we can let flow out into our lives by cultivating a joyous spirit.

It does not matter so much what our experiences are as how we react to them. This is what is definitely important to our well-being, to our health, happiness, and success.

What are your reactions to life? Have you analyzed them?

How do you react when something disturbing or unexpected happens?

Do trivial things bother you?

Are you in control of your emotions?

Do you dramatize the negative aspects of your experiences?

Many of us may hold to the thought that some persons are naturally happy and that other persons are naturally moody or despondent. This is not true. What, then, keeps us from being joyous individuals? It is our reactions to occurrences in our life that cause us to be happy or unhappy.

No matter what happens, let us "count it all joy." Let us be joyous in every experience and pray to find the blessing in that experience. For the outgrowth of habitually dwelling on the idea of joy is happiness.

What can we do about our reactions? Can we change them? Yes, we can change them. The power of thought is the power of control. It has been said that "our destiny changes with our thoughts." We shall become what we wish to become, do what we wish to do, when our habitual thought corresponds with our desire.

When you are enshrouded in gloom, you can do something about it. If you have been depressed, unhappy, anxious, hurt, or disappointed, you do not need to wait for a certain turn of events in order to become joyous again. The change can come through a change in your thinking. Even in the midst of gloom, drop a thought of joy into your mind and you will begin at once to get a joyous reaction. Like the ripples that extend out and out when a stone is dropped into a pool, even one thought of joy reaches out and out into your entire life and starts a joyous reaction.

A word of joy that has meant much to me is this: *"Christ within me is my glory. The brightness of His presence casts out all darkness, and my whole being is full of light."*

When we touch the inner spring of joy, we feel the strength of it constantly sustaining us, no matter what may seem to go wrong in the external world.

True happiness is not dependent on conditions. It is not dependent on other persons or on things. It derives from our attitudes of mind. True happiness is an outgrowth of developing the habit of joy.

But often we think of happiness as dependent on only one word—*when.*

We may say: "When I get into a new home—" "when I can buy a new car—" "when I can take a vacation—" "when I get well again—" "when my husband stops drinking—" "when something happens—" "when something changes—" "when someone changes—then I shall be happy!"

A mother may say, "I'll be happy when the children are in school." Later on, she says, "I'll be happy when the children are out of school." Then when the children are grown and out of school she says, "I was so happy when the children were little and in school!"

We must cultivate and increase our ability to enjoy life today; then the very spirit of happiness will accompany us tomorrow. Our capacity to enjoy life increases as we use it.

William Allen White, at the age of eighty, wrote:

"I have never been bored an hour in

my life. I get up every morning wondering what new, strange, glamorous thing is going to happen, and it always happens at fairly regular intervals. Lady Luck has been good to me, and I fancy she has been good to everyone. Only some people are dour, and when she gives them the come hither look with her eyes, they look down or turn away and lift an eyebrow. But me, I give her the wink, and away we go."

Self-centered persons find it difficult to be happy. All of us have known persons who feel sorry for themselves, who are unwilling to overlook hurts and slights or the words and actions of those with whom they disagree. These persons have harbored thoughts of self-pity and injustice until they have become veritable clouds of depression.

Have you formed any of these negative habits and long to be free from them?

When we are in a state of gloom, we think that no one treats us right. We see other persons who are happy and we think: "Well, he has never had any trouble, but just look at me. My whole life has been one great disappointment after another."

Some persons are inclined to believe that anyone who is happy is selfish and has lived a life free of trouble or care. But when we come to know the truly happy person, we find that he is not happy because of better conditions but because of his attitude of mind.

The one who radiates happiness is not always the one whose life has been carefree. He has learned to cultivate happiness and joy and enthusiasm for living; he has met the challenges of the day and become master of himself.

All of us can learn to transcend conditions; we can learn to control our moods and our reactions to life; we can learn to make joy a habit. We can be the kind of person we want to be. The power lies within us. We may not have a great deal of

understanding, but we can use what we do
have. As we take even one idea of Truth
and live with it and work with it, as we
refresh our mind daily through prayer, we
awaken our divine nature, and a transformation begins to take place within us.

Ideas of Truth are stabilizing and helpful. It may be the thought, *"All things
work together for good."* Or it may be an
affirmation such as, *"I am poised and centered in the Christ Mind, and nothing can
disturb the calm peace of my soul."*

Ideas such as these can become a basis
for right reactions; they can help us to keep
our thoughts centered in the right direction.
They can give us a focus for our energies
so that we no longer fall into gloom, depression, or even despair.

Life is yours to enjoy. You can control
your moods and your reactions to life. You
can make joy a habit!

How to Be Young—Spiritually, Mentally, Physically

L<small>ET ME</small> ask you a question. How up-to-date are your ideas about your life? How do you feel about it? There is nothing closer to you than your life.

We are now living in the space age, constantly expanding our ideas about it. We are literally tapping the secrets of the universe. But are we getting any new ideas about bringing up to date the man who is to live in this new age?

We spend millions of dollars studying ways and means to promote better living conditions, so that we can live in an up-to-date world. Almost every city in the country has had its face lifted, and the country is criss-crossed with superhighways and the sky with airways. Remodeling goes on and on. We remodel everything but ourselves!

A few years ago Unity was unique in its teaching about the enduring, eternal quality of life. Now, many men of science are coming forth with these same ideas. For instance, David Sarnoff, chairman of the board of Radio Corporation of America, has said we seem to be tapping everything except our vast spiritual vitality. He claims that material progress is a delusion unless we put it to the service of eternal spiritual values.

Life is one of our most important divine attributes. We should accept the responsibility of learning about its character and putting it into expression.

Another scientist, Dr. Donald Hatch Andrews, whom I referred to in the chapter, "Keeping in Tune," has made some revealing statements about the forces and atoms in man's body. He is spending his life in atomic research and understands the forces about which he speaks. At a Rotary convention in Dallas he stated: "Our new knowledge brings us new hope, for the same experiments that are giving us atomic power are also giving us atomic vision. We can look inside the atom and see something beyond the material. We can see through to a new horizon of Spirit."

He explained that if a tiny atom of calcium from the tip of the bone of one of our little fingers was enlarged a few trillion times so that we could stand inside of it, this is what we would see: At the center of the atom we would see a central light, around which lesser lights that we call electrons are circling, like the planets in our solar system. The tiny whirling point of light at the center of the atom is the atomic sun.

Now we are commencing to understand that our body is composed of millions upon millions of these atoms, at the center of each of which is light and energy.

I believe that the Christ at the center of our being is our true sun around which we revolve. In the light of this understanding our hearts are stirred with a joyous response which is felt in every atom, cell, and force of our body. Then with David we can say:

"Bless Jehovah, O my soul;
And all that is within me, *bless* his holy name."

For we realize how much more there is to the "all that is within me" than we had formerly thought.

People say, "I would not want to live forever." No, we would not want to live forever in limited bodies and in our present limited state of consciousness. But most of our ill health, both physical and mental, is caused by our lack of understanding of the true nature of life. You see, we limit ourselves to the human concept of life. We think of life as limited rather than as endless, eternal.

"God created man to be immortal and made him to be an image of His own eternity."

We need to establish a new premise

about life and to work from that premise. For instance, our premise could well be one like this: "Life is continuous and eternal. The life I live and am aware of at this moment is Godlike, eternal life." With an idea like this on which to base our thinking we shall come into a new understanding of the limitless, eternal life within us. We shall come to know that there is never any end to life.

In spite of the scientific discoveries being made about man's capacity for enduring life, man has held on to a very limited concept of life.

One scientist has said: "We are only half awake. The individual lives within his own limits."

Even though man has a limited concept of life, he has always wanted to live. Even though he submits to death because he believes that it is God's will for him, more than two thousand years ago Ezekiel saw with a flash of inspiration that God says to man, "I have no pleasure in the death of him that dieth . . . wherefore turn yourselves, and live."

Whether we are able to prove eternal life is a different story; but as we turn ourselves and live, as we implant the idea of eternal life in our consciousness, we shall experience a different feeling and a different quality of life and thus start a rejuvenation of ourselves.

In an article, "You May Live Forever," William J. Laurence tells us that the findings of scientists reveal that there is within the human being the possibility of renewal and immortality. He speaks of the "sculptor of life" which "hibernates" in the body after the process of growth has been accomplished. He says that those of us now living have the possibility of making a second birth in the body, and within fifty or a hundred years we will be doing so, and the body will be renewed so that we can live as long as we like.

Surely these thought-provoking ideas are a challenge to us. We accept startling new scientific discoveries, but it seems hard for us to accept ideas that change our old way of thinking about ourselves.

Where did our life come from? The origin of our life is in God. He breathed into us the breath of life, and we became living souls. Surely God thinks of us as He created us, surely He sees His children as living expressions of His life. We need to learn to think of ourselves in the way that God thinks of us.

What are some of the limited concepts of life that keep us from expressing a fuller consciousness of life, from enjoying life?

Are we limited by what we think we have inherited? Do we blame heredity for ill-health, lack of vitality, some specific disease?

We need to take hold of the idea that life is unlimited, ever-renewing, eternal, enduring. We need to take hold of the idea that our inheritance is from God, that we are children of God, that we have within us His life, His love. God is the source of our life, our energy, our health. We are set free from the bondage of erroneous belief when we continually affirm our freedom, when we claim our divine birthright and when we accept ourselves as children of God.

Have we felt bound by time, have we accepted the idea that our allotted time is three score years and ten?

We should always keep in mind that man uses the system of counting days, years, and centuries to reckon progress, but the time system is man's idea, not God's. We can rise above the thought that we are bound by time by knowing that there is no time in Spirit, that we live in the eternal now.

Perhaps we feel tired, run down, discouraged, but entertain the hope that next week or next year we shall have more life and energy. Now is the time to do something about this attitude of mind. Now is the time to draw upon the life of God. We live in it, move in it, have our being in it. The power to resurrect is not a supernatural power. In each cell and atom of the body there is life, substance, and intelligence. We speak a word of life, and every atom and force in our body responds. We can charge the atoms of our body with life, eternal life. They are always listening, always receptive. If we present the idea of life to our body it takes up this idea and acts on it. The idea works through the cells and atoms of our body and generates life and energy.

This was the way Myrtle Fillmore blessed her body into the fullness of life. She called life forth in every part of her being by praising life. And her body responded and she was healed.

The teaching that life is eternal is one of the teachings of Jesus and one of the basic teachings of Unity School. When Jesus said, "I am the resurrection, and the life," He knew His identity as a son of life without beginning and end. The only life we have, the life that flows through our body this moment, is eternal life.

Some people say to us, "I am too old to take up these ideas." But our consciousness about life starts in the mind, and we are never too old to think!

That mental power does not decline with age was proved by Dr. Irving Lorge, eminent psychologist of Columbia University. Doctor Lorge's results from working with an intelligence test devised by Edward L. Thorndike showed that though mental speed declines slowly with the years, mental power never declines at all, that it may even increase with expanding knowledge. His results show that if you could solve a problem in business or science or government or human relations when you were twenty-five, you can solve it just as well even up to ninety years of age.

In an interview George Bernard Shaw, at the age of ninety, stated: "Death is not to be regarded as natural and inevitable. We die because we do not know how to live and kill ourselves by our lethal habits."

Let us forget the idea of growing old and commence really to live. Let us be like the woman who when the doctor said: "That pain in your leg is caused by old age," replied: "That's nonsense. My other leg is the same age, and it doesn't hurt a bit." We should not let inactive ideas clog the mind, but let new, creative, life-giving ideas express themselves in and through us.

When we go along in the same old way for a long time, we may find it a little difficult to act on new ideas. We need to get into the habit of acting on our ideas.

Let us act on our impulse to express love and joy and friendliness; let us act on our impulse to do good to our fellow man; let us act on our desire to make good, productive changes in our way of living.

Let us make up our mind that we are not going to let ourselves get into a rut. Let us not be afraid to make changes in our life, to try new things, to attempt to do something that is new and challenging.

So many of us sit and watch life go by. We sit back and think that we have no part in it. The youthful person is never content simply watching other persons do things. The youthful person tries to do things himself. The youthful person wants to take part in activity. We need to cultivate the habit of action, the habit of becoming a part of the picture rather than merely watching life go by.

It is not so much what comes into our life that matters as what we do about it. We have the ability to take life as it comes and make something of it.

We should not let inactive ideas clog our mind. One of the things that classifies us as old is thinking of all the happiness and good things as being in the past and longing for the "good old days." Living in the past is a sure way to become old.

Let us stop asking people how old they are. In a recent article by a doctor, I read: "No woman should tell her age. It is bad psychology." If people insist on knowing how long we have lived, I will tell you one way we can give them a good answer. We can say: "I have been here throughout eternity, and I expect to stay. A lifetime is only a flash in eternity."

In order to stay young and active we must find new interests, we must create within ourselves a love of life; we must be willing to try new things, we must be willing to take part in life.

We need to say to ourselves, "I dare to be young!" We cannot be young unless we feel young. It is not the way we dress or the way we act that makes us young. It is our consciousness of life, youth, and joy that determines this. Life is consciousness, and we express life on the level of our consciousness. When we understand life from the standpoint of consciousness, we realize that what we think, what we feel, and what we believe makes up our consciousness and becomes our life's expression.

Any one of us can learn to love life, to love people, to love beauty. Any one of us can stir up a new spirit of interest and enthusiasm.

If you start to think of yourself as being too old to make a new start, check yourself, for this is merely an excuse for not making a new start. Make up your mind that you are not going to stay in a rut. Youth is a matter of attitude, not of calendar age. Instead of thinking about life running out, affirm this idea: *"I am alive, alert, awake, joyous and enthusiastic about life,"* or *"I am the ever-renewing, ever-unfolding expression of joyous life and youth."* Do not talk about your rheumatism, your poor eye-

sight, your failing health. Remember that
there is "yet more to be found" within you,
that the very source of life is within you,
renewing you in mind and body. Your
wonderful body accepts what you tell it.
So, tell it the truth. You are young, strong,
and healthy. It will respond to these ideas.

We cannot live life to the fullest unless
we begin to live now. We need to lay hold
of life now, to stir up new interest and
enthusiasm, to let go of fear and limiting
beliefs. We need to know that we have the
life of God in us now, that at this moment
we are living in the very midst of eternity.

"God created man to be immortal, and
made him to be an image of His own eternity."

Complete in Thee

A Meditation

THERE IS no frustration, no loneliness, no longing in my heart that Thou, O Father, dost not satisfy and fill to overflowing through Thy great love.

There is no sadness, no depression, no limitation in my life.

I am complete in Thee, satisfied in Thee.

I seek Thee with my whole heart; because I so earnestly seek Thee, I find Thy comfort, Thy strength, Thy peace here with me now.

Because of my completeness in Thy love I freely relinquish all the things that are unimportant in my life's experience. They are forgotten, forgiven, and released.

I release everything of the past that no longer contributes to my happiness. I release any apprehension for the future. I live in the joy of the present.

I hold fast only to that which is of the very highest and best, enduring and enriching.

Every condition, every individual adds to my joy because I have first found Thee.

The joy of my oneness with Thee knows no bounds.

I radiate to every person I meet the joy that comes through my completeness in Thee.

There is peace in my soul and there is harmony in my affairs because I know Thy love.

I place my life in Thy hands without care or anxiety about the future, for I know that all is well.

Thy love satisfies my longing soul and fills my life with Thy good.

What Are You Afraid Of?

ARE YOU afraid of the future? Are you afraid of people and their opinions? Are you afraid of ill health, of lack, or of loneliness? Are you fearful of some known condition, or are you fearful of unknown conditions and things? These are fears common to most people.

We can live and enjoy life without fear, you know! Most fears take to their heels if we do something about them.

Jesus gave us the idea of building a substantial foundation for a fearless life in these words: "Every one therefore that heareth these words of mine, and doeth them, shall be likened unto a wise man, who built his house upon the rock: and the rain descended, and the floods came, and the winds blew, and beat upon that house; and it fell not: for it was founded upon the rock."

We cannot always reason ourselves out

152

of fear. But we can always be one who "heareth . . . and doeth" the bidding of the Christ within. We can always pray and work our way out of fear.

When we recognize fear as an emotion having little to do with the circumstances or conditions with which we are faced, we find it easier to handle. Very often we are unable to put our finger on our fear; we cannot say what we fear or why we fear it. We are simply filled with fear. We are afraid of our own weakness. We fear that we are not equal to life and its demands.

I have seen people cringe before a thunder storm. I have known individuals to shake with fear when a telegram was handed to them. I have known other people so full of worry that when they went to bed at night they could not sleep because of the depressing fears and the gnawing anxieties they had allowed to stay in their minds. Then, in the middle of the night, they have awakened feeling alone

and helpless because of they knew not
what.

One friend wrote to the Silent Unity
prayer group: "For the last year I have
been so full of fear that I really can't see
where there is any fear left for anyone else;
fear of disease, fear that what little we
have will be lost in a lawsuit now pending;
fear of losing my mind, even. Yet I am
absolutely certain that the great Father of
love is much more powerful than any of
these, if one is only able to consciously contact that Source."

Of course, this was Silent Unity's opportunity to pray with our friend. She
learned to be one who listens for and
"heareth" the Christ indwelling and "doeth" His bidding. And soon she was free
from fear.

The power that controls the emotions is
within. The power that frees us from fear
is within. Think of the way Jesus took
command in His own life's experiences.

Undoubtedly He also had to deal with His thoughts and emotions, but His approach was always positive and practical. Jesus knew that "greater is he that is in you than he that is in the world." He knew that through the Christ within all power is given unto man.

Do you remember the story of the apostles awakening Jesus when they were in the boat on the Sea of Galilee? They were caught in the midst of a big storm, and the winds and the waves were making a surging, turbulent sea. The apostles awakened Jesus crying: "Teacher, carest thou not that we perish?" Jesus rebuked the wind and the waves. He spoke from the Christ within, and there was a great calm. So we calm our emotions and disturbed states of mind by speaking peace from the Spirit within. When we speak: "Peace, be still," we find that the wind and the waves of our emotional nature subside.

Little anxieties have grown into fears

because we have allowed them to. We did nothing to stop them. Since God has given us the power to control our thinking and our feeling by placing His Spirit within us, we are not supposed to let our thoughts run riot. We should never involve ourselves in negative conditions. We should involve ourselves emotionally, and with all that is within us, in those things which are constructive and upbuilding.

Dr. Henry C. Link, author of the book, "The Return to Religion," writes in Readers Digest: "I venture to say that at the bottom of most fears, both mild and severe, will be found an overactive mind and an underactive body. Hence, I have advised many people, in their quest for happiness, to use their heads less and their arms and legs more—in useful work or play."

In counseling with a young man who was in need of peace of mind, Doctor Link pointed out: "You have put too much of your physical energies into thinking and imagining things. If you run hard enough, you will automatically relax and go to sleep. You have thought yourself into this fear with your mind, you can run yourself out of it with your legs." Doctor Link further states: "And he did."

All of us have had something disconcerting happen to us, something not too important, but something that was disturbing; then we became busy with something else that interested us and we soon forgot what we had been anxious about.

We have built many negative emotional reactions into our consciousness, and they have left their mark on our subconscious mind. Then, because we have done nothing to correct these feelings, the little fears and anxieties have gathered together and they make a big fear complex.

We arouse the victorious, overcoming Spirit within, we put our physical and mental energies to constructive use, through teaching our consciousness the truth. The truth is that we are God's beloved children. We are fully endowed, through His Spirit within us, to handle every situation that confronts us. By referring often to this indwelling Spirit we gain control over fear. We realize that as we travel in this orbit of Spirit there is nothing to fear.

Peace and serenity are not found in a set of circumstances and conditions in life. Peace and serenity come through a feeling of oneness with that which is eternal and secure. That feeling is established and becomes permanent through daily prayer. As we daily build thoughts and feelings of peace and serenity into our consciousness we are building our life on a stable foundation.

Nehemiah, the prophet, said of the Jewish people rebuilding the walls of Jerusalem: "The people had a mind to work." Every overcoming depends on a "mind to work." It is in speaking the word that we need to have this mind to work. We need to be persistent in prayer. Then we find we have the inner strength and courage to meet life's experiences and walk through life as all-conquering men.

No matter what your fear may be— even the fear of death—remember that God has taken care of you throughout eternity and you can trust Him to continue to care for you. You can affirm with Paul: "For I am persuaded, that neither death, nor life, nor angels, nor principalities, nor things present, nor things to come, nor powers, nor height, nor depth, nor any other creature, shall be able to separate us from the love of God, which is in Christ Jesus our Lord."

There is no power in negation. Power is of God, and God is good and God is love. What can stand against the power that holds the world in its hands, the power which created you in its own likencss, and gave you the authority to command in your own life's experiences?

You can live and enjoy life without fear. If you have been fearful, know for yourself: *"There is nothing to fear. I trust God in all that concerns me. 'The Lord is the strength of my life; of whom shall I be afraid?' "* Then act as though there is nothing to fear. Act as though you trust God in all that concerns you. Act as though the Lord is the strength of your life.

If you have been fearful for your dear ones, place them lovingly in God's care. Use a prayer like this for them: *"I place you lovingly in the hands of God. He protects you. He watches over you."* Then act as though you have placed them in God's care. Act as though He is protecting your loved ones and watching over them. Follow through on your faith.

Develop stability in your emotions through the practice of prayer. Keep your mind stayed on God, the good, until you build up the consciousness of God, the good, in your nature. Use the idea: "Thou wilt keep *him* in perfect peace, *whose* mind *is* stayed *on thee.*" Put it in the first person: *"I am kept in perfect peace because my mind is stayed on God."* The power of this idea will radiate in and through every part of your life. The power of this idea will enable you to be fearless.

A meditation, like the following, will help you to keep in tune with God and His goodness by forming the habit of remembering your close, intimate relationship:

"I am the loving Christ Spirit within you. I have been with you from the beginning of time. I shall continue to be with you throughout eternity. If you will but tune your ear to listen to Me, I will guide you safely through every experience of life.

"No matter how many times you may have stumbled along the way, I have forgiven you and put you back on your feet.

"I surround you with My love so that you may have a feeling of security.

"I am the loving Christ Spirit within
you. Let Me heal your mind and your
body. Let Me heal your heart when something troubles you. Turn your anxieties
and your fears over to Me. I will give you
peace.

"I will harmonize and adjust all your
reactions to life's experiences. You need
not worry or fret. Go happily on your way.
Accept Me as the constant, loving presence
with you, and I will not fail you. Learn of
Me, trust Me."

Some Lenten Thoughts

THROUGHOUT the church world during the season of Lent people strive to become better Christians, and this season of fasting and prayer means much to all of us if we enter into its observance in the right spirit.

Some concentrate their attention so strongly on a state of penitence during Lent that they find themselves unable to rise into a happy resurrected state of mind by Easter. We should not look upon the Lenten season as a forbidding one or a sad one. It should not make us unhappy to give up what is not for our benefit. But let us, as Truth students, be joyous during this Lenten season and inspire others to be joyous also.

We find such words as these especially associated with Lent: sacrifice, renunciation, self-denial, atonement, and penance. However, these words are not so forbid-

163

ding as they sound at first.

When we give up a bad habit we are not losing anything. We are merely getting rid of something that retards our progress. There is nothing in such an action to make us sad!

If a person has a tendency to gossip, to say ugly things about a friend, if he is deceitful in his attitude or dishonest in his dealings, renunciation of such practices is surely good.

In Truth we daily practice renunciation through denial and affirmation. We deny that which we do not desire in life and claim that which we do desire. Renunciation is a stronger, more dramatic word than denial, but it in effect means the same thing.

Denial and affirmation are equivalent, also, to fasting and prayer. Fasting is denial, and prayer is affirmation. Fasting does not always refer to abstinence from food, but to abstinence from material gratification of any kind that might hinder spiritual unfoldment. This sort of abstinence is a spiritual means of observing Lent.

Lent is a time of self-discipline, and members of some churches find it expedient to restrict the physical appetite and to restrain mental impulses and tendencies. Following this practice does not bind us in any way, but brings us greater liberty as sons of God.

If you have been eating too much, Lent is a good time to restrain your appetite, through prayer first, of course. If you have a bad temper, Lent is the time to restrain your impulse to "fly off the handle." If you have a tendency to nag, to criticize, or to find fault, Lent is a good time to give up the habit and to improve your disposition.

Each of us surely is aware that he has something he needs to improve upon. Lent gives us opportunity to decide on what needs improving, and to be honest with ourselves. It is a time of self-discipline,

through which there is nothing to lose or
be sad about but everything to be gained.
We never let go of anything unworthy of
us without immediately making room in
our mind and heart for some better thing
to enter. Denial of the personal self brings
us into greater unity with the divine self—
God—and the attainment of such unity is
what we desire.

We all want greater freedom as sons
of God, but we sometimes imprison ourselves by giving way to selfish desires. The
self-indulgent man is really a slave to his
desires. Only he who is master of his desires and impulses is free.

In their Lenten observances, some
churches speak of the mortification of sight,
the mortification of hearing, and the mortification of the tongue—that is, the disci-
plining of these faculties.

Here is a prayer that we can use to
help us to watch these things: *"Through
the Spirit of truth within me I know,*

see, hear, and speak only Truth."

During Lent let us reconsecrate our eyes, our ears, and our tongues to Truth. If we have observed wrongly, if we have been seeing with the "double" eye, seeing both good and evil, let us see Truth. If we have been listening to idle tales and criticism of others, let us commence to hear only the Truth, only that which is constructive and uplifting. If we have been speaking disparagingly of our neighbors and fellow workers, if we have talked about sickness, poverty, and inharmony and thought of these as realities, let us commence to speak Truth.

We do this through the help of the Spirit of truth within us, not through our personal will. Especially are we quickened to the help of the Spirit of truth within us during Lent. For Lent is a period of prayer and spiritual preparation. There is a spiritual power at work during Lent that backs us up in our desire to overcome.

Through the Spirit of truth within us we see all people as radiant, all-glorious, beautiful, free sons of God, unfettered, unbound, triumphant, rising supreme out of every trial. What wonderful things there are to see when we see with the single eye of Truth!

Through the Spirit of truth within us we hear glad tidings of good. We hear of people healed, people prospered. We hear the message God has given to us, because our ears no longer want to hear ugly things about anyone. We hear celestial music and we feel in tune with it, because our ears are tuned to hear infinite harmony.

Through the Spirit of truth within us we are able to speak the word that brings forth health, happiness, and prosperity. We are not lending our tongue to negation, criticism, or faultfinding. We are speaking words of Truth.

Jesus said, "If any man would come after me, let him deny himself, and take up his cross, and follow me." Let us deny the claims of the personal man, overcome his sorrows and shortcomings, and follow the Christ.

This is the purpose of Lent: To permit us to reconsecrate and rededicate ourselves to the will and the work of Jesus Christ; to permit us to gain freedom from bondage to the personal man; and to triumph in the liberty of the sons of God.

"We come to Thee, O Lord, in silent
    prayer;
Our hearts to Thee, our hearts to Thee
    Are open now. Amen, Amen."

Some Facts about Lent

The word *Lent* comes from the Anglo-Saxon word for spring, which is derived from a verb meaning "to lengthen." Lent comes in the spring, when the days become noticeably longer.

This annual season of fasting, prayer,

and penitence has been observed by the western Church since the first century after Christ, although it has not always been forty days long. In more recent times it has been kept forty days, after the example of Moses and Elijah, and above all to commemorate the forty days of fasting and prayer that Jesus spent in the wilderness.

The first day of Lent is called Ash Wednesday from the custom that prevailed in the early church of sprinkling ashes on the heads of penitents on the first day of Lent in token of repentance for sin.

Ash Wednesday comes forty-six days before Easter. There are six Sundays in Lent, but they are not considered part of Lent because in the western Church Sunday is always a feast day. The forty weekdays following Ash Wednesday constitute Lent.

The last week of Lent is called Holy Week. It includes Palm Sunday, Maundy Thursday, and Good Friday.

Palm Sunday, the Sunday before Easter, commemorates Jesus' entrance into Jerusalem when the people strewed palms in His way.

Maundy Thursday, the Thursday before Easter, commemorates the Last Supper.

Good Friday, the Friday before Easter, probably known originally as God's Friday, commemorates the crucifixion of Jesus.

Easter Day, of course, commemorates the Resurrection. The word *Easter* comes from the Anglo-Saxon word *Eastre,* the name of the goddess of spring, in whose honor a festival was celebrated each April. Easter Day always occurs on the first Sunday after the full moon that occurs on or after March 21. If the full moon falls on a Sunday, Easter is the next Sunday. Easter can never occur earlier than March 22 or later than April 25.

Your Importance to God

HAVE YOU ever thought how one-sided our attitude toward God is? We expect God to be alert to our every need, to answer our every prayer instantly, and to recognize our every good thought. Yet how few of us are alert to His presence and power, how few of us recognize the answers to prayer when they do come, how few of us express His intelligence, His love, and His goodness!

When you wonder why God does not answer your prayers, ask yourself: "Am I answering God's thought about me?"

Co-operation is part of the divine plan. God is important to us, and we are important to God, for we are His conscious expression.

Whether or not he realizes it, man has a definite spiritual purpose in life. Thousands upon thousands of persons have not yet awakened to this purpose and have not

172

found a way out of their discouragement. Life, to them, is a routine process from birth to death.

Our purpose in life is not just to live, not just to rear a family, not just to be a banker, a doctor, a lawyer, a storekeeper, or a businessman. These are all secondary purposes. The first purpose for which God created us is to express Him, to develop our spiritual character.

When we become aware of this primary purpose, then we can put something real and alive and useful into our secondary purposes and become successful men and women.

All the frustrations, anxieties, and problems that distract us and seem so real and important exist only because we have not recognized our spiritual nature, because we have not drawn upon our spiritual resources in meeting circumstances and conditions.

Sometimes an individual suffers from

the belief that he is a sinner and God cannot forgive him. Through the modern-day psychiatrist we hear a lot about "guilt complexes." The psychiatrist has brought many persons to Unity's door because after analyzing a patient's mind and life he is not always able to show him what to do to overcome his problems.

Someone has said, "A saint is a sinner who keeps on trying."

A story has been told about a couple who took their small boy with them when they visited Europe. As tourists do, they visited many cathedrals on the Continent and in Great Britain. On their return the little boy was in Sunday school when the teacher asked, "What is a saint?"

The little fellow remembered the many cathedral windows he had seen and replied, "I know; it's a man that the light shines through!"

There was a woman who had been a drug addict for years, but through the study of Unity she was able to free herself. However, she suffered from a guilt complex and condemned herself to a point where she was constantly ill. She was free from the drug habit but not from the feeling of self-condemnation. She did not feel that God could forgive her for her past failings.

She was told to think of God as the principle of good instead of a Being who was constantly holding something over her. God, the principle of good, is always loving, always without condemnation. Who can imagine a principle of mathematics becoming angry and punishing us because we fail to use it correctly? Neither does God, the principle of good, condemn us. The woman grasped this idea and felt free from illness for the first time in years.

Our greatest sin is holding onto what we have thought of as our sin and not going forward because of it. Jesus did not think of sin as unforgivable. He said, "Thy

sins are forgiven . . . Thy faith hath saved
thee; go in peace."

Carrying around with us the belief in
sin is what makes neurotics of us. Our real
sin is our lack of faith in the unchanging
goodness of God.

How do we increase our importance to
God? Through daily prayer, which is the
sincere effort to know God.

If you feel unimportant, you can build
up an inner strength, stability, and confidence that you have never felt before by
making an affirmation such as the following, which is one of Silent Unity's favor-
ites: *"I am the radiant, all-wise, all-loving,
all-conquering son of God. I rule supreme
in all the affairs of mind and body. Infinite
wisdom guides me, divine love prospers
me, and I am successful in all that I under-
take."*

To know your oneness with God, your
divine sonship, is one of the greatest helps
in proving your importance to God.

There was a miner in Colorado who got into difficulties and suffered greatly from self-condemnation. Someone sent him an article by H. Emilie Cady. He got one special idea out of the article, and it was this, "God loves me and approves of what I do." And it was this new idea of himself, of God's thought about him, that saved him from self-destruction.

What is true of God is true of you as a son of God, but you have to believe it and prove it. You are a part of God Himself, and He needs to express Himself through you. Let Him! Appreciate Him as love and life. Praise Him as the good you want. Love Him as the source of all good.

Besides the special meetings and the continuous prayer ministry of Silent Unity, Unity School has a prayer group dedicated to blessing our work and our workers. This group is led by a different worker each month. One month the prayer group leader shared this statement with us in the meeting of all the workers: "Lord, make me a productive channel." And certainly as we pray to become productive channels for God, we are letting Him express Himself through us in a way that is important to God and to man.

Thousands of persons write to Silent Unity each month to tell us that they could not bear to face life's problems without the help of God. God is important to them, and whether they realize it or not, they are important to God.

Harry Emerson Fosdick once said in a radio talk that the individual may not feel important but the ideas he stands for can change the world. Great ideas start with the individual. Do not believe in futility; believe in the possibility of great ideas. Open your mind, let God's wisdom express itself in you. Open your heart, let His love express itself in you. Open your mouth, give His word expression. The word of God is mute unless expressed through man.

Sometimes people ask, "Am I good enough to express God?" Yes, you are good enough, because you are God's own child.

"Beloved, now are we children of God, and it is not yet made manifest what we shall be."

God loves you and approves of you. God needs you, His own beloved child. You are very important to Him!

A Practical Approach to Prosperity

"IN THE beginning God." These are the first words in the Bible, and if you will remember in the beginning of everything you do that God is with you, guiding, directing, and inspiring you, you will be prospered.

In the beginning of your life there was God; in the beginning of your day there is God. If you remember always to turn to God each day for inspiration and help, the right ideas will find expression through your consciousness.

This is the way it will work perhaps: you will be meditating on the wonderful thought of the omnipresence of God and you will think about His life, His love, and His substance manifesting themselves through you. All at once you will say, "I have an idea!" The idea, born of God, will be a rich one, and you will be assured of ever-increasing prosperity and success.

In the Bible some very definite laws governing prosperity are given. Solomon, David, Jesus, Paul, and many other illumined ones have given us spiritual laws to follow in attaining prosperity.

These laws are not true just because they are in the Bible. Rather, they are in the Bible because they are true. They have lived through the ages. They have been tried, not only by these great teachers but by many of their followers, and they have been found to provide the perfect solution to the problems of thousands.

Let us consider three of these laws for prosperous living. The one of first importance was given by Solomon when he said, "Give thy servant therefore an understanding heart . . . And God said unto him, Because thou hast asked this thing, and hast not asked for thyself long life, neither hast asked riches for thyself, nor hast asked the life of thine enemies, but hast asked for thyself understanding to discern justice; behold, I have done according to thy word: lo, I have given thee a wise and an understanding heart . . . And I have also given thee that which thou hast not asked, both riches and honor."

Apply this law that Solomon invoked in all your affairs. If your business needs a turn for the better, ask for an understanding heart. Whatever your need, your first need is for understanding. Then other things will follow.

For definite instructions in providing for your needs, read the 6th chapter of Matthew. This chapter is especially helpful to anyone who has fears concerning food, clothing, or shelter. Jesus tells us not to worry about these things, that the Father knows our need. And He gives us a law to follow in gaining prosperity. This is the second of the laws I mentioned: "Seek ye first his kingdom, and his righteousness; and all these things shall be added unto you." What could be more definite?

Take this instruction as the key to the solution of your problem now. "Seek ye first his kingdom." Jesus tells you that the kingdom of God is within. The idea that controls things—food, clothing, shelter—is within you. God's kingdom is one of rich ideas within you. Within you is the starting place of all the forces of your being. The life within you is God life; the love within you is God love; the power within you is God power; the substance within you is God substance; the judgment you use is God judgment.

When you seek the kingdom of God, you are seeking to use your love, your life, your judgment, your power, your imagination as they should be used, righteously.

Seek the source of your spiritual forces within and then use them, recognizing that God is their source. Use your love to bless, your faith to inspire, your strength to encourage, your imagination to picture only good. Then you will have no need to fear

that you will not be fed, clothed, or shel-
tered. For as Paul says, "Eye hath not seen,
nor ear heard, neither have entered into the
heart of man, the things which God hath
prepared for them that love him."

The third law of prosperity is to be
found in the 22d chapter of Job: "If thou
return to the Almighty, thou shalt be built
up . . . Then shalt thou lay up gold as dust,
and the *gold* of Ophir as the stones of the
brooks. Yea, the Almighty shall be thy de-
fence, and thou shalt have plenty of silver.
For then shalt thou have thy delight in the
Almighty, and shalt lift up thy face unto
God. Thou shalt make thy prayer unto him,
and he shall hear thee . . . Thou shalt also
decree a thing, and it shall be established
unto thee: and the light shall shine upon
thy ways."

The Bible is full of laws governing
prosperity, and practically all of them have
in them this same idea: return to the Almighty; then "thou shalt . . . decree a

thing, and it shall be established unto thee."

Prosperity, to be permanent, must come through us. If we could be given prosperity without a rich consciousness, such a gift would be contrary to spiritual law.

As we build a prosperity consciousness through thinking, developing rich ideas, and using all of our potentials and abilities, we find that we are stabilized in a permanent prosperity consciousness.

We may experience many conditions of temporary prosperity that we cannot maintain until we have been awakened from within. This is one reason why inherited wealth so easily slips away from some persons. It is the reason that giving outer help, such as food and lodging, to other persons is seldom effective except in emergencies.

One thing we need to remember about the prosperity laws is that each individual must prove them for himself. In the home the wife cannot have the consciousness for the husband, nor the husband for the wife. Many times a wife frets because her husband does not make more money. What is she doing about the situation? She should develop her own rich consciousness, and then she will be a blessing and an inspiration to the household. One person can help another through prayer, but he cannot do all the work for him.

Every individual must develop his own rich consciousness. Let us not fret about anyone else, but develop our own inner resources.

Many times the man of the home feels overly responsible for the whole family. Each person is entitled to be independent and to learn to demonstrate his own good. Children are necessarily the responsibility of the parent, but even children should be taught to look to God for their supply and support. They should be taught that their supply comes from God and is always where they are.

As paradoxical as it may seem, in order to be established in a state of well-being, one must turn loose, temporarily at least, in consciousness the things that represent prosperity to him.

We loosen our hold on things in order to lay hold of the understanding of the law that governs all things. Then when we understand the law better we take a stronger hold on what we desire.

Most of us at some time have had the experience of thinking we were at the end of our rope. Then, when we turned loose of the rope through letting go of our intense hold upon situations or things, we grasped a whole new understanding of life. Let us remember that nothing leaves our lives except to make room for something better.

At certain stages of development, houses, lands, money, things can become a "graven image." We may love them so much that for us they take the place of the one true God. In fact, some persons may become so confused and discouraged when they have to give up something that has become a "graven image" to them that they feel they would rather die than to continue to live without the desired possession.

Jesus says, "Where thy treasure is, there will thy heart be also."

"Seek ye first his kingdom, and his righteousness; and all these things shall be added unto you." Your faith works to form the perfect conditions desired. And praise is one of the powers of mind you must not fail to use, if you would be prosperous. Praise neither affects nor increases God, but it enlarges your own consciousness so that you can receive largely. Refuse to see poverty or disorder. Hold to the idea that you are abundantly prospered and praise God as the source of all.

You deserve to be prospered, for you are a child of God, and every child of God has a right to be rich!

On Wings of Prayer

CHARLES FILLMORE was frequently asked, "How do you account for the phenomenal growth of the Unity work?" He had this question in mind when he wrote:

"What really is the technical or detailed explanation of the law that we put into action? I should say that from the very beginning of our work everybody connected with Unity was asked to make prayer the keynote of every act. We have literally fulfilled the command, 'Pray without ceasing.' We prayed without ceasing; and the older the work gets the more we pray. . . . Not only do we pray without ceasing but Unity readers the world over are asked to join us every day in our class prayer."

The Fillmores chose for the symbol of Unity not the cross, which to so many persons represents the suffering of Jesus, but instead, they chose the winged globe, which represents the relation existing between spirit, soul, and body. Through the transcending power of Spirit man's soul and body take wings. And it is through prayer that man's spiritual nature is aroused.

Unity's greatest contribution to the field of prayer is its emphasis on the affirmative prayer. It is in contrast to the petition, "O God, give me this, if it be Thy will," which implies that perhaps God's will is negative. In Unity we emphasize the prayer of decree or agreement; however, the affirmative prayer is not unique with us. Jesus used the affirmative prayer. Isaiah and many of the other prophets of old used this type of prayer. For instance, this prayer of David is an affirmative prayer:

"Mine eyes are ever toward Jehovah;
  For he will pluck my feet out of the net."
Or this one from Isaiah:

"Behold, God is my salvation; I will trust, and will not be afraid: for Jehovah, *even* Jehovah, is my strength and song; and he is become my salvation."

Many affirmative prayers use the I AM identification. For instance, *"I am the ever-renewing, ever-unfolding expression of infinite life, love, and wisdom."*

Prayer works. The thousands of letters we receive weekly in Silent Unity testify to this. Prayer moves upon mind, body, and affairs and heals, adjusts, and prospers. We believe that Silent Unity is successful in its ministry of prayer because we are organized for constant prayer.

Perhaps you have never tried the efficacy of prayer, or perhaps you have tried it and have not found the good results that you expected immediately. Then perhaps you have thought, "Why pray?" You pray to appropriate food for your soul.

As you pray, you generate the spiritual energy that renews and heals you in mind, soul, and body. One of the important things about prayer is that it awakens and

arouses within you the self that is capable
of standing, regardless of what comes. A
good affirmation is this, *"Through the
Christ in me my spiritual nature is now
aroused."* The use of such an affirmation
awakens within you the knowledge that the
Christ in you, as it was in Jesus, is closer
than breathing, that "in him we live, and
move, and have our being."

"They that wait for Jehovah shall renew their strength; they shall mount up
with wings as eagles; they shall run, and
not be weary; they shall walk, and not
faint."

The waiting upon the Lord comes before the mounting up with wings. We usually interpret this as meaning: "I've said
my prayer, and now, Lord, I'm waiting.
What are You going to do about it?" And
usually the waiting is very impatient waiting.

To wait upon the Lord means to tune
our consciousness to the presence of God,

to wait for that animating presence which is within and all about us, ready to reveal itself.

When we take time to wait upon the Lord, to commune with Him, He reveals Himself to us as the answer to our need. The outer thing we think we need may not be immediately forthcoming, but we shall discover that "they shall mount up with wings as eagles" is symbolical of our ability, gained through prayer, to rise into a higher and freer and happier way of life. We rise on the wings of prayer into a realm of joy, and we retain the beauty of the experience in every act of our lives.

What steps should you take in order to find health? You should turn to the Lord. You should wait upon the Lord. He will inspire you with ideas of life and strength and peace as you recognize Him as the source of life within you. In the beginning He breathed into you the breath of life, and He is continuing to breathe through you as the breath of your life.

Acknowledge God as renewing, invigorating life, expressing itself in every part of your being. If you wish to abide in the strength that never grows weak or weary, acknowledge God as your unfailing strength.

Commune with God, talk with Him, and He will say to you, "I will; be thou made clean." Accept willingly in your mind the healing, and it will express itself in your body. Agreement in your body consciousness is necessary; then the very atoms and forces of your flesh respond.

After you have made your inner contact with God, after you have opened your mind, your heart, and your soul to His outpouring of love, make a simple affirmative prayer for health, such as this:
"God is my health, I can't be sick;
 God is my strength, unfailing, quick."

Where we need to strengthen ourselves is in the realm of mind, into the depths of which we have poured all types of negative beliefs. When we do not get quick results in the body, we must change our thinking. So we say: *"I am open and receptive in every phase of my mind to God-given ideas. I meet in agreement with the truth of my spiritual nature. Thoughts of the past that have held me in bondage to negative conditions of any kind are entirely erased, and from this time forth I meet in agreement with the ideas of my spiritual nature that build constructive conditions in my body."*

Nothing is expressed in the body that has not had access to the consciousness through the mind. Opening the mind to fully accept the truth of your spiritual nature is like opening a door. All the true ideas about your strong, healthy body flood the cells and atoms of your flesh. There are no closed doors in the body consciousness. All the work is done in the realm of mind —and when the doors are open to the

health, vitality, and life of the spiritual
realm, God's Spirit floods your entire being. It renews, revitalizes, rebuilds, and
heals every part of your being. Through its
operations you are reborn into an entirely
new life.

If you want right results and answered
prayer, you must co-operate in every way
with the ideas embodied in your prayers.

If you are praying for peace, be peaceful; if you are praying for divine order, be
orderly. Remember that prayer changes
you. It brings you to the place where you
are working with your prayer for its right
fulfillment. You are responsible for at least
half the answer to your prayer.

We frequently pray for some good
thing, but we continue in the same old
grooves; we continue with the same feelings we had before our prayer. For this reason Silent Unity emphasizes the idea of con-
tinual practice of the presence of God.

If in your prayer you are not getting

the answers that you desire, let me ask you this question, "How are you getting along with yourself?" You will notice that I did not ask, "How are you getting along with your family, your job, your business associates?" But "How are you getting along with yourself?"

When you get so that you criticize your wife, your husband, your children, your associates, and everything else, you need to answer the question, "How am I getting along with myself?"

Study your attitudes, your outlook. Are they true?

Recently I read a book on prayer that emphasizes the idea that all of us have need for the prayer of conversion, the prayer that changes our character. Conversion means, in its simplest form, giving up the false for the true. It means completely surrendering the old, false habits for the new and beautiful way of life.

We need conversion not only for the

healing of mind and body but for the changing of the disposition and for the upliftment of the whole being. We cannot experience conversion and retain the old, false thoughts. Our prayer is for the purpose of changing us, not the other fellow, circumstances, or conditions.

The idea of trying to change other persons through prayer without changing ourselves reminds me of a story about a man who visited the Ozarks and asked a native for directions. He asked, "Is this the road back to Kansas City?"

The native answered: "Not exactly. This road moseys along for a ways, then turns into a hog trail, then it turns into a squirrel track, and finally it runs into a scrub pine and ends in a knothole."

And so it is with any prayer that does not deal with changing ourselves for the better. It gets us nowhere.

The quickest and best way to experience conversion is to follow the teachings of

Jesus who not only said, "I am the light of the world," but also said, "Ye are the light of the world."

The Christ in you says, "I am the light of the world." As you follow the light of Christ within you, you will never be in darkness. You will walk upon an illumined path and rise on wings of prayer into a new and glorious life!

Come Ye Apart Awhile

JESUS knew the value of going apart, not only from the multitudes who were following Him and His disciples, but He also knew the necessity of getting away to the mountains to pray.

If Jesus, with all of His developed spirituality and control of earthly things, knew the value of going away by Himself, how much more important it is to you and to me to get away from the bustle and hustle of daily living to seek the quiet place where we can relax and pray.

I do not believe that Jesus' retirement from the multitudes meant merely that He wanted to get away, but He understood the importance of increasing His own spiritual powers through prayer.

We are learning that we need to take time each day to go apart and arouse the powers and possibilities of our inner nature through prayer.

It is well to establish the habit of prayer by meditating at the same time each day. This helps bring order into the prayer practice. If we leave this important prayer period of the day until everything else is accomplished we are apt to neglect it.

When circumstances and conditions in the home and in business become too pressing, it is well to withdraw more often to the mountaintop, away from the decisions and responsibilities which are confronting us. Then we find the strength and wisdom needed to handle easily all the experiences of life.

We develop the powers of the spiritual nature through prayer. As the inner strength of the spiritual nature is quickened and unfolds in us, all of life becomes ordered. We put into action those higher laws which are innate in every man, and each one of us becomes the conquering man.

We find, as it is so beautifully expressed in the lines of one of the old hymns, "and where there seems a desert, the rose shall burst in bloom."

Ideas for growth and development are written in the heart of every man. Jesus referred to the place we seek as "the kingdom of God . . . within you." Jehovah spoke through Jeremiah, the prophet, and put the same idea into these words: "I will put my law in their inward parts, and in their heart will I write it."

Through quiet moments of prayer we open our mind to the wisdom that has been written in our heart.

Many persons ask us to teach them how to relax, how to meditate, how to *How* pray in order to become healthier, *to* happier, and more successful in *relax* their daily living. We approach the art of meditation and prayer first through learning to relax completely in God.

Now as a first step in the practice of relaxation, we acknowledge one presence and one power—God, the good omnipotent. Then we quiet our thoughts and our emotions by saying: *"Be still, and know that I am God."*

We think about God's love surrounding, infolding, and protecting us. We feel very close to God. We abide in the idea that "underneath are the everlasting arms." No evil shall befall us.

Meditate on these ideas for a few moments, and you will feel a great sense of peace. Say to yourself: *"I relax in mind and body. I feel the peace of God. I rest in His loving presence."* Think of surrendering your entire being to God—spirit, soul, and body. Take a deep breath, relax, and let go.

As a part of the relaxation phase of this drill we like for you to think of relaxing in every   *Relaxation* part of the body.

First direct your whole attention to your feet. Think how wonderful they are to support your body. Think relaxation in the arch of your foot. Think perfect balance into the entire foot. Let go of any feeling of being cramped or tense. Think relaxation in the backs of your legs, up the calves of the legs, and under your knees.

Think of the small of your back and up and down the spine. Say: *"Relax and let go."* Then say: *"I am relaxed and I feel relaxed."*

Think of letting go through the shoulders. Some persons literally push themselves out of the body by thoughts of hurry and anxiety. Release the shoulders and settle back into your body, the wonderful temple of God.

Feel relaxed in every part of your body. Relax your neck and the back of your head. Now, as you read this, feel relaxed.

Through the forehead and between the eyes, relax and let go. Remind yourself that you are relaxing into the harmony and peace of the presence of God, that in God you live, move, and have your being. Relaxation comes to your mind and body through a feeling of trust in the presence and power of God.

Continue with the thought of letting go of all tension, thinking especially of the throat and chest, then the solar plexus, then through all the organs and functions of the body, down to the tips of the toes.

Say: *"I am free from tension, stress, and strain. I surrender myself entirely to God. I am at peace in mind and in body. From the top of my head to the soles of my feet, I feel relaxed. I am calm, serene, relaxed. I feel God's peace filling my mind and my body. I rest in God."*

The first part of this drill has been for the purpose of relaxation. Through relaxing you have pre- *Purpose* pared the way for an outpouring *of first* of the Holy Spirit into every part *part of* of your being. Eventually through *drill* the practice of daily prayer, we shall find ourselves always attuned to the

Spirit of God within. This is the goal we
are seeking, to live always in the consciousness of the presence of God, and to
follow through in all of life's activities in
the awareness of unity with God.

As we learn to turn more and more
often to the Spirit of God within for direction, our lives become less burdened,
more carefree and joyous. It is wonderful
to follow the direction of the Spirit of God
within us. To relax and rest in His presence
puts us in harmony with all life.

Now we will take up some positive
words of renewal for the entire body. With
your attention at the top of the head, let
us use these words of Jesus: *"I am the light
of the world."* He not only
Realization said, "I am the light of the
world," but also, "Ye are the
light of the world." Think of the wonderful radiant light of the Christ. See it shining through every part of your being. Feel
that you are all aglow from the top of your

head to the soles of your feet. The body is composed of trillions of atoms and at the center of every atom is light. We are commencing to realize that we are not mass and material, but that we are essentially spiritual substance, light, and intelligence.

Center your attention in the forehead, between the eyes, and say *"Not my will, but thine be done."* Meditate upon this idea and be freed from willfulness.

Bless your eyes with the words: *"Blessed are my eyes, for they see clearly, distinctly, and perfectly."*

Through the relaxation part of the drill you have already freed your eyes from tension and strain, and when the strain is removed your eyes respond quickly to the idea of seeing easily and clearly.

Follow the same idea with your ears. Say: *"I am God's loving and obedient child. Blessed are my ears, for they hear easily, clearly, and distinctly."*

With the attention directed to the

throat say: *"All power is given unto me in mind and in body."*   .

Many times we let conditions and circumstances rule us, instead of asserting the spiritual power and mastery that are within us. Power is given to man in his spiritual nature; and, when you recognize and use the power that is within you, you will be freed from anxiety and from confusion in your world.

Now with the attention at the back of the neck say: *"I am not bound in personal consciousness; I am free with the freedom of Spirit."*

A phase of personal consciousness we want to be free from is that which tries to direct the lives of other persons into some particular pattern we have made for them. Relax. Release other persons and their affairs. Turn them over to the loving care of God. Love your family and your friends, but let their own indwelling Christ direct them.

Also, when we are free from personal consciousness we are free from the tendency to gossip, to criticize, or to take offense. These are surely phases of personal consciousness from which we wish to be freed.

Think again of your shoulders and say: *"My yoke is easy, and my burden is light."* Then imagine a yoke of light extending from your chest around your shoulders. Make it a yoke of light in your imagination. Place your burdens in the light of Christ, and they will be dissolved.

With your attention at the small of your back affirm: *"I am strong in the Lord and in the power of His might."* You will immediately feel your back straightening up.

Now turn in loving thought to your lungs and say: *"There is nothing to fear. I breathe the breath of life freely and easily."* Breathe deeply and be at peace.

With your attention centered at your heart, bless this wonderful organ, intended as an instrument through which the love of God is to be expressed. We have placed many burdens upon the heart. Let us free it now by accepting the forgiving love of Jesus Christ. With your attention toward your heart say: *"The forgiving love of Jesus Christ sets me free from mistakes of the past, and the results of mistakes of the past."* The power in the name of Jesus Christ will free you from remembering the mistakes of the past. It will reach the very depths of your being. It will cleanse and purify your heart. Now feel that God's love, a pure stream of love, is flowing in and through your heart, and through your blood stream, cleansing, healing, purifying, and restoring your entire body.

Use these words: *"God's cleansing, healing, purifying love flows freely through every part of my body, renewing and restoring me."*

Think of the functions of your body and affirm divine order. *"Divine order is established in my mind, body, and in all my affairs."* Remember that our thinking is always from center to circumference. We first think of divine order as an idea in mind, which has action through the body, and then out into the world of affairs.

Think of the wonderful life of God that animates you, and fills you with enthusiasm and energy. All life is of God, so the life you are feeling this very moment is the eternal life of God, expressing itself through you, vitalizing every part of your body.

With the attention on the lower part of the body affirm: *"The life of God is from everlasting to everlasting, and I live, move, and have my being in it."*

Say for the whole body: *"I am the ever-renewing, the ever-unfolding expression of infinite life."*

Say this many times and feel the response of renewing life and energy in the body.

A scientist has said that if the atoms in the palm of the hand could be released there would be enough energy to power all the utilities of a city.

Jesus knew the secret of releasing the energy in His body; He resurrected it from death and continues to live in His original spiritual perfection. He fulfilled His promise, "Lo, I am with you always."

"And he saith unto them, Come ye yourselves apart . . . and rest a while."

Dare to Believe!

"THEN SHALL thy light break forth as the morning, and thy healing shall spring forth speedily." How wonderful it is to understand and accept this promise for one's self.

Besides this power-filled text from Isaiah, there are many healing promises found in the Old Testament. Jehovah spoke through Ezekiel, saying: "I will put my Spirit in you, and ye shall live." Truths like these have been depended upon by people throughout the ages and are even more universally accepted now.

Jesus Christ, understanding the Scriptures, having faith in the Truth they reveal, made healing an important part of His ministry. He declared His faith in healing when He said: "All things are possible to him that believeth."

I have always liked the affirmative statement: *"This I believe."* For in the many experiences in life which confront us, we need to take a positive stand. We need to believe.

I have always believed in the healing power of God. I was brought up in a family where belief in the healing power of God was fundamental. We were taught to depend on prayer in every act of our life. We were taught to pray always in all things.

When I say: "This I believe," my saying these words is based on the experience of seeing healings of all kinds, in the family and out of the family. My father was a charter member of Unity Society and was a steadfast believer in the healing power of Jesus Christ. He wholeheartedly believed in Truth as taught by Charles and Myrtle Fillmore. He constantly expounded the Unity teachings, in the Unity Sunday school, in his home, and in his business. What he believed was never far from his thought and was ever a part of his expression and his actions.

In this background I grew up and into the Silent Unity work.

In Silent Unity, the prayer ministry of Unity School, we hear daily of the healings of hundreds of persons. If all who ask for prayer do not experience full and complete healing, all are illumined and blessed and awakened to a new idea about God and His love for them.

At some time in our experience it is necessary to sort out the facts from the fancies upon which we build our lives and come to a faith that we can accept as entirely dependable. To believe that something is true and to say: "This I believe," does not imply a closed mind. It implies a stabilized mind.

The ideas we believe in today can constantly expand and grow in our consciousness. What we believe about God should steadily grow and expand, for all the truth about God has not yet been discovered.

However, if we can develop a strong belief in God as eternally good, we can build a strong foundation for our life.

Dare to believe! Put what you believe into action. This is the challenge. Belief must become action if you are to realize healing—if you are to put the most into life and get the most out of life.

If your present belief in God is not bringing you health, happiness, and peace of mind, perhaps you have not yet grasped the true concept of God as the working power in your life. Get a closer look at God as He expresses Himself through you, through your mind and your body. Think of God as the very Spirit within you. God is not only the Principle of good, working in the universe, God is the Spirit of good working in and through you. Direct your attention to this warm, loving Spirit of God, and something vital stirs within you; you commence to feel this Spirit as your very life. It is light. It is life. It is love.

It is health. The thrill of life and health aroused renews and restores your body.

After you have wired your home for electricity you do not go outside to the transformer to turn the lights off and on. You turn to the electrical current that is in your home. You press a button, you turn a switch, and the light is there where you need it. Likewise, when you desire a greater feeling of the presence and power of God in your life, you need not go outside yourself. You make contact with God's presence and power by turning within in quiet prayer. In His abiding place within you, you find His light, His life, and His love easily accessible.

When we have the correct concept of God, we can, even as Jesus did, dare to believe that "all things are possible." Do not become confused by terms. We frequently speak of "the I AM that I AM." You remember that Jesus said: "Before Abraham was born, I am." At another time Jesus

said: "It is the spirit that giveth life."
Paul spoke of "Christ in you, the hope of
glory." In these statements the terms are
different but the meaning is the same. In
our prayers we use the name of Jesus
Christ, Christ in you, the Spirit of God,
and other terms. There are many names for
God, and every person should use the name
that means the most to him, the name that
makes him feel closest to God, the name
that brings him the clearest concept of God.

Jesus used Himself as a symbol of the
universal Christ. The things He did He
counted on every man to do. He counts on
you to do these things.

Sometimes the question is asked: "Am
I good enough for God to heal me?" Yes,
you are good enough. You are good. The
Christ is in you, for the Christ is in every
man. Never think of yourself as unworthy.
You are the beloved child of God and you
can be forgiven, cleansed, and healed
through His indwelling Spirit, the Christ

Spirit. The moment you turn to the Christ within, the radiant light of His recognized presence sets you free from past mistakes, and you are lifted up in consciousness so that you know that you have the same Christ in you that Jesus had. You are a son of the living God.

You will recall the story of Peter and his recognition of Jesus as the Christ. Jesus asked His disciples: "Who say ye that I am?" And Peter, who was commencing to see the truth, said: "Thou art the Christ, the Son of the living God."

The lesson for us in this experience is that through an illumined faith the Christ, the Son of God, will be revealed to us. When this recognition comes to us our healing springs forth speedily.

Healing is the keynote of the Unity ministry. The Unity work has grown and prospered and now reaches around the world because of the healing idea. Healing includes mind, body, and affairs. In fact, healing includes everything that relates to man.

The healing work of Unity is done as Jesus admonished—"in my name"—in the name of Jesus Christ. For this healing ministry is based on the teachings of Jesus Christ.

Unity teaches a way of life, a way of thinking, a way of feeling, and a way of praying that brings man to the full attainment of his Christ potential.

Unity believes that man's need for healing arises because he has lost contact with, lost the awareness of, his spiritual nature. This contact is restored, this awareness quickened, through daily prayer.

From the writings of the old prophets we gather that they kept faithful contact with God. In many instances the Old Testament states that Jehovah, or the Lord, spoke through various illumined ones, and they in turn related to their people what was revealed to them.

The Lord spoke through Isaiah, saying: "The Spirit of the Lord Jehovah is upon me; because Jehovah hath anointed me to preach good tidings unto the meek; he hath sent me to bind up the broken-hearted, to proclaim liberty to the captives, and the opening *of the prison* to them that are bound; to proclaim the year of Jehovah's favor."

Isaiah was attuned to listen to the message of God that was spoken through him. Later in the New Testament it is written that Jesus also recognized this truth as spoken through Him.

"And he came to Nazareth, where he had been brought up: and he entered, as the custom was, into the synagogue on the sabbath day, and stood up to read. And there was delivered unto him the book of the prophet Isaiah. And he opened the book, and found the place where it was written,

"The Spirit of the Lord is upon me,

Because he anointed me to preach good
       tidings to the poor:
He hath sent me to proclaim release to
       the captives,
And recovering of sight to the blind,
To set at liberty them that are bruised,
To proclaim the acceptable year of the
       Lord.

"And he closed the book, and gave it
back to the attendant, and sat down: and
the eyes of all in the synagogue were fas-
tened on him. And he began to say unto
them, To-day hath this scripture been fulfilled in your ears."

In this instance, as in the instance of
Jesus' questioning of Peter, we see that He
was fully conscious of His oneness with
God and He could freely proclaim the fulfillment of the promise made to Isaiah.
Jesus was so sure of the truth of His spiritual nature that He knew this scripture was
fulfilled in Him. Our spiritual nature must
also be aroused to this place of belief, so

that we can say: "Today has this scripture been fulfilled in me," and "The Spirit of the Lord is upon me, and it radiates through me as healing power."

We are growing and developing in our spiritual nature and we should commence to proclaim boldly the truths of the Scriptures. To proclaim these truths we do not need to wait until our consciousness has developed to the fullness of the Jesus Christ consciousness. Right where we are we should use the Truth that we know and understand to heal the sick and to set free men who are bound in negative thoughts, opinions, and conditions.

Healing in the name of Jesus Christ is taking place every day, not only in the Unity ministry but in many churches and in the field of evangelism.

For over seventy years Silent Unity has been a center of a healing work. Our "room of light" is known the world over. It is a symbol of healing—healing in the name of

Jesus Christ. Every day hundreds, yes, thousands of persons find spiritual illumination and new beginnings through the ministry of Silent Unity. Through this ministry we emphasize that God is a present help and that no one is separated from the love of God.

People who do healing work love God and love their fellow men. This love is the connecting link between man and God. This love releases the healing stream of life that flows through us to do its renewing, rebuilding, restoring work.

Jesus, again referring to the Old Testament, emphasized the importance of love. In the gospel of Luke we are told that He bade the disciples to go out and preach the gospel. He assured them that the harvest was ready but that the laborers were few. He encouraged them to heal the sick and to say to them: "The kingdom of God is come nigh unto you."

Then we read: "Behold, a certain

lawyer stood up and made trial of him, saying, Teacher, what shall I do to inherit eternal life? And he said unto him, What is written in the law? how readest thou? And he answering said, Thou shalt love the Lord thy God with all thy heart, and with all thy soul, and with all thy strength, and with all thy mind; and thy neighbor as thyself."

Then, we are told, Jesus said to the lawyer: "This do, and thou shalt live."

Jesus' answer, given in response to a query concerning the attainment of eternal life, is also the answer to the healing of men's minds and affairs.

Many persons speak of their great faith, and they cannot understand why they do not receive their healing. Faith by itself is not enough. Paul stressed "faith working through love." Add the divine quality of love to your illumined faith so that it may produce the results you wish in your life. For without love even an illumined faith

is cold. It takes love, warmth, and understanding to bring about healing. Peter
(faith) took John (love) with him when
he healed the lame man at the Temple gate.
Take warm, loving compassion with you
into your prayers for healing for yourself
and others.

There are many methods of healing;
each method contributes its specialty to
the general field of healing. Spiritual ideas
are the basis of healing in the Truth way.
Spiritual ideas are healing! When an individual is awakened and comprehends the
truth of his spiritual nature, he realizes
that healing must come—not from without
himself—but from within himself. He
glimpses the truth in Paul's instruction:
"Be ye transformed by the renewing of
your mind." The transformation of the
mind, of which Paul speaks, comes when
man is awakened to the idea of himself as a
spiritual being. This awakening is indeed
the "truth" of which Jesus spoke: "Ye

shall know the truth, and the truth shall make you free."

A part of the mission of Jesus Christ, as a universal symbol for the race, is to show man the truth of himself as a spiritual being. Jesus came to reveal man's true nature and to lead man to an acceptance of eternal life. We all recognize the eternality of spirit, but we have a great goal before us. We want to lay hold of Jesus' idea about redeeming the body.

In our daily lives we function mostly from what we speak of as the natural man, or the body man. Ill health comes because there is a lack of co-operation in man with his spiritual nature. In order to come into an idea of wholeness we must quicken and arouse the spiritual nature within us. The idea of ourselves as spiritual men gradually becomes the dominating idea in our mind. When it does, our lives are no longer affected by the impulses or ideas that bind the natural man.

As we learn to pray with an idea of our spiritual nature in mind, we release powers and energies and forces that heal mind and body.

We learn to think of the body as an expression of the spirit in us. We learn to think of every atom of the body as filled with life and substance and intelligence.

Science tells us that man's body is a body of light. At the center of every atom there is a nucleus of light which may be called an "atomic sun," and there are trillions of atoms in man's body. When we commence to think of our body as spiritual, this idea of a body of light helps to dispel the thought that the body is dense, heavy, and material.

If we take the attitude that we are a spiritual being, that we constantly take our direction from Spirit, our body adjusts itself to this new education. The body rejoices in knowing and hearing and responding to the Truth we teach it.

We are told in Job: "And all the sons of God shouted for joy." Think of all the atoms in your body as "sons of God" that shout for joy when you tell them the truth of their spiritual nature. Your body rejoices to be told the truth of its spiritual nature. It rejoices to be told that life is eternal. It rejoices in this eternal life of God which is constantly circulating in and through every part, doing its healing, restoring work.

When you speak your words of Truth about your body, make a mental agreement with these words. Many people pray with their lips, but do not put feeling into their prayers. Make an agreement with the ideas about which you are praying. Not only say your prayers, but feel them. When the point of agreement is made and the subconscious phase of mind takes up the ideas, "healing shall spring forth speedily."

The next time you pray a healing prayer, try doing it in this way, with this affirmation: *"I send my healing word to the depths of my being, and every atom of my body accepts it and responds. I am cleansed, purified, and made new. The atoms of my body shout for joy. This I decree in the name of Jesus Christ."*

When we pray in this way, we are not making healing too much of a personal effort. The pressure of stress and strain and trying hard does not bring about healing. Healing comes through releasing oneself entirely to God.

Speak your healing word for yourself and for other persons, then release all anxiety about results.

The words of Whittier's poem, "The Healer," make this idea very clear:
"So stood of old the holy Christ,
    Amidst the eager throng,
 With whom His lightest touch sufficed
    To make His people strong."

Keep in mind that when we are in the Christ consciousness the "lightest touch" brings healing. When we are in the Christ consciousness we learn to give all life's experiences this light touch. We do not lend the substance of our thought to dramatizing aches and pains or the need for supply. With Paul we minimize what we do not want by knowing, "None of these things move me." Then nothing can shake our faith in our divine nature and in the responsiveness of our body and affairs to the word of Truth.

From this time forth accept the light and life of God as your own. Know you have God's Spirit, the Christ Spirit, within you. Know that through this Spirit you can do all things. Dare to believe! Put your belief into action. Accept yourself as Jesus Christ accepted Himself—as a son of the living God. Speak your word in the name of Jesus Christ. Start where you are. Love God. Love people. Love yourself. Love life. Your faith works through this love. Believe in eternal life. Think of your body

as an expression of eternal life. Tell it that
it is an expression of this life so that it may
rejoice in this knowledge. Come into complete agreement with the words of Truth
that you speak. Then you will know as Paul
knew, that you "have put off the old man
with his doings, and have put on the new
man, that is being renewed unto knowledge
after the image of him that created him
. . . Christ is all, and in all."

Dare to believe!